A Little Help
from My Friends

If Walls Could Talk
Christmas at the Mansion
Don't Let the Fire Go Out
The Tide Always Comes Back

A Little Help
from My Friends

...and Other Hilarious Tales
of Graying Graciously

JEAN CARNAHAN

*former First Lady of Missouri
and U.S. Senator*

Vantage Point Books and the Vantage Point Books colophon are
registered trademarks of Vantage Press, Inc.
FIRST EDITION: February 2012

Published by Vantage Point Books
Vantage Press, Inc.
419 Park Avenue South
New York, NY 10016
www.vantagepointbooks.com

Manufactured in the United States of America
ISBN: 978-1-936467-23-5

Library of Congress Cataloging-in-Publication data are on file.

9 8 7 6 5 4 3 2 1

Cover design by Victor Mingovits

Contents

Introduction

It took me seventy-seven years to figure out life, but with the help of my friends Edna and Verna, I've done it. Together we've tackled the aggravations of aging the only way we knew how—with sunny abandonment. Within these pages, we react to everything from malls, manners, and makeup to birthdays, beauty secrets, and bras. We take on underwear, handbags, clutter, airport security, grandkids, napping, habits, pets, health, saleswomen, travel, coffee shops, and weddings. We are opinionated and vociferous.

Too many older adults look upon their life as a shrinking island to which they retire surrounded by their aches and pains, regrets, disappointments, and fears. By contrast, we are three gutsy septuagenarians with a hearty outlook on life. Like ancient seers, we have found the answers to the perplexities of daily living and we are eager to share our insight. In addition, we review various products we have discovered that lessen "senioritis" or, at least, make it more tolerable.

I might mention that other than my satire-laced, political blog (http://www.firedupmissouri.com), this is the first of my humorous writings to take on book form. Until now, I have been far too serious. As first lady of Missouri in the nineties, I wrote a five-pound coffee-table book about the history of Missouri's first families and followed that up with a colorful cookbook. After leaving the U.S. Senate, I wrote an autobiography, *Don't Let the Fire Go Out*, and in 2009 I released a collection of inspirational essays entitled *The Tide Always Comes Back*.

Now I am taking a more fanciful course, giving advice and writing absurdities—a pursuit that Dr. Seuss advocated because it "wakes up the brain cells." I am joined in this venture by two wonderful make-believe friends, Edna and Verna. They are a "friend-blend," a composite of many people I have known over the years. When relatives or friends ask if they are in my latest book, I reply, "Yes, you are—in Edna and Verna's DNA."

When it comes to aging, the three of us recognize that you can't turn back the clock—though you can rewind it. Hopefully, a few laughs and some hearty recollections will encourage you to do some stem winding along with us.

Keep ticking.

Jean Carnahan
St. Louis, Missouri, 2011

Shimmering Lips, Waddling Hips

My kids once gave me a certificate for a facial, but I never used it. I find it annoying to have anyone fiddle with my face. That includes the bubbly sales clerks in the department stores who spot me several counters away and want to perform their magic on my countenance.

I recently made a trip to the mall to replace my lipstick. It was an emergency purchase; the rim of my old tube was beginning to leave scrape marks on my lips. In my haste, I wandered into one of those makeup boutiques with the strobe lights and the funky sales clerks with spiked hair and nose rings. As I browsed the cosmetic collections, I thought I had inadvertently stumbled into a porn shop. One shelf was labeled Plump Your Pucker and another—I kid you not—was called Super Orgasm. I got out of there as fast as my titanium hip joint would take me and headed for my old standby, the anchor store at the far end of the mall.

I was out of breath by the time I arrived in the familiar surroundings of Macy's cosmetic department, a space that covers nearly a half acre of the store's layout. I collected myself before approaching a counter, determined to stay focused on my mission.

"I need a tube of Pink Paradise lipstick," I said quickly to the clerk in the black smock with the perfectly tinted face.

"I'm sorry," she replied sympathetically, "but we haven't carried that shade since 1997. You must have had a large supply on hand."

I was downcast. I began to argue, insisting that I had bought the tube within the last several years. The young lady smiled softly and introduced herself as "Tiffany," a professional cosmetic artist happy to assist with my facial needs.

"Do you want to be dramatic, sexy, or bold?" she asked as she commenced her reprogramming session.

"None of the above. I just want to keep my lips from falling off, looking like fish scales, or taking on the appearance of a cadaver."

Tiffany said the newer products would modernize my appearance, giving me healthier, more full-bodied lips with a shimmering, multidimensional illusion of depth.

My mind paused momentarily, like a jammed printer flashing an overload signal.

"Does Margaret still work here?" I asked.

"No, Margaret retired last month. I'm caring for her old clients," she said with a detectable emphasis on the word "old."

"Drats," I said to myself. "Margaret would have found my color from a stash of old favorites hidden away for discerning customers like myself and I'd be out of here lickety-split." Desperate and running out of options, I begrudgingly submitted to my new lip care provider. I hate to buy cosmetics that require a training course, but I succumbed. I fell respectfully silent as Tiffany commenced her tutorial.

She selected various tubes from her array of samples and applied several colors to the back of my hand. Pointing to one of the smudges, she declared, "This product complements your skin tone and has far more conditioning properties than what you're getting now." She said the new lip color would moisturize my lips, protect them from harmful UV rays, add natural collagens for a plumper look, and stay on, possibly, ten minutes longer than my old brand.

During the next forty-five minutes, I learned that lips need extra moisture because they have so few oil glands. I learned the difference between a matte finish and a gloss. I learned that Celebrity Sexy Pout is the pick of serious lippies and would earn me two to three compliments a day. If I wanted longevity (of lip color, that is), the hands down winner was Max Factor Lipfinity. Elizabeth Arden

Exceptional "is to die for" she crooned, "rich and smooth, but you have to apply it almost hourly."

To complement my new look, Tiffany introduced me to a number of lip accessories, including moisturizers, balms, plumpers, and vitamin gels. She said that an outlining pencil and brush were essential for disguising lip wrinkles and achieving an even layer of color that wouldn't wander onto my chin. She concluded by showing me how to blot correctly on a tissue to set the color, but not blur it.

Tiffany said if I would come in again, she'd make my eyes look ten years younger. I told her a plastic surgeon had offered me twenty years, a tempting proposal but not one covered by Medicare—yet.

As I bonded with my new lip coach, I couldn't resist passing on a story someone told at my bridge club. "Did you hear what happened at a middle school in Oregon?" I asked. "The girls would blot their lips on the bathroom mirrors and every night the custodian had to spend extra time scrubbing it off. Finally, the principal assembled the girls in the bathroom to allow the custodian to show them how much trouble it was to clean the mirrors. He took out a long-handled squeegee, dipped it into a toilet bowl several times and scrubbed the mirrors clean. Since his demonstration, there have been no lip prints on the mirrors."

"Yes," she said with a patronizing smile, "I've heard that story several times. I think it's an urban legend." I could tell

Tiffany was too close to her own teen years to find the tale as humorous as had the women in my bridge club. But as long as I had a cosmetic expert at my fingertips, I delved further.

"The women in my bridge club brought up a tantalizing question recently," I said. "Do you have any idea how many tubes of lipstick the average woman has eaten in her lifetime—you know, on food and with lip licking and such?"

Obviously, she had touched on that topic in her facial studies because she didn't hesitate in the least.

"We eat a lot less than we used to since we now have light lip glosses that give just a hint of color."

"I guess it's best we never know for sure," I said with a sigh as I handed her my credit card. She agreed. I went on my way, leaving Tiffany to change the world one set of lips at a time.

Now each time I wear my new color, my daughter says, "That's such a warm subtle shade; it's just right for you." I am so pleased. On the other hand, a number of friends my age have looked at me and said, "Why aren't you wearing lipstick anymore?"

But Edna, who knows me best, ignored the amenities. She stared at my collagen-rich lips and said, "I hate to say this, Jean, but your lips are beginning to swell and so are your ankles. I think it's time you go back on your diuretic pills."

"I Came, I Saw, I Conquered"

I am unaccustomed to the luxury of a first-class international flight. Happily, it allows me ample space for the trappings of leisure travel: books, magazines, newspapers, pillows, blanket, headset, and, of course, the complimentary beverage and travel kit provided by the airline.

I was unprepared for the stewardess who interrupted my nest building. She seemed weary already, as if she might have pounded the aisle of a jumbo jet on too many transatlantic crossings. Unlike the younger, cheerier crew members, she had service stripes on each arm to symbolize her longevity. Her neatly placed pocket hanky and name tag gave her the look of Flo from *Mel's Diner*.

She had a trained smile, which she clamped on while bending to my eye level as one would when addressing a small child. I forced a return smile. We distrusted each other instantly.

"What would you like?" she asked, as if I should know.

"What do you have?" I replied.

She knew my type—snarky and flippant. "It's all on your menu. Have you read it?"

"No, I've been settling in," I replied.

"Then I'll be back," she huffed and hurried off to be of help elsewhere. Fortunately for Flo, sassy Edna was not there to comment. She was checking out the powder room, as she usually refers to the women's restroom, and later pronounced it hygienic but cramped.

Edna and I were on our way to Venice, Italy. Harry didn't want to go. It was just too much trouble to leave home, he claimed. So Edna left him behind to care for the cat. Besides, Harry said that he saw too many cities sitting in water during the flood of '93; he didn't need to pay to see more. Even so, he insisted that we travel first class and we didn't argue. So, it was late March and we were two little old ladies on a European holiday.

I scanned the menu before Flo made her return round and selected my entrée—which one gets to do in first class. All other items were literally à la carte. There was the drink cart, the appetizer cart, the bread cart, the fruit cart, and the dessert cart. If I ate from each, they would have to cart me off the plane.

As soon as the dinner trays were whisked away, the cabin shifted into sleep readiness. Although it was only nine p.m., seats reclined and eye shades and blankets appeared. Cabin lights and window shades were downed and Flo and her associates disappeared into the bulkhead. We were in snooze mode for all of four hours before we were tricked into waking up at two a.m. (body time), force-fed breakfast, and exposed to sunlight on the other side of the world.

I raised my window shade and looked out onto the snow-capped Alps far below. In a moment of dazed reflection, I murmured to Edna, "How do you suppose Hannibal got his elephants over those mountains?" I immediately knew I had asked the wrong person.

"Maybe it was summer," she said nonchalantly, taking a sip of her V8 juice. When I rolled my eyes, she offered better advice. "Why don't you Google it? You brought your laptop, didn't you?" Yes, I had packed my computer because Harry, who had booked the hotel, said there would be a wireless connection.

Later that morning when we arrived at the hotel, we discovered an additional bonus. We had a balcony with a panoramic view of the waterway with its fleet of motorboats, water buses, and gondolas. Just below our window, peddlers were selling souvenirs, delivery men shuffled carts, and students with backpacks vied for space with luggage-laden tourists along the busy walkway. The falling value of the dollar caused Americans to be scarce, but Japanese and European tour groups abounded. They passed beneath our balcony in droves, each led by a guide with a colorful pennant.

One guide stopped to explain the gigantic statuary of a horse and rider outside our hotel. I leaned over the rail to listen and learned that the bronze horseman was the first king of Italy. As the guide spoke, her flock scattered like a gaggle of geese, taking pictures quickly before running to catch up with the group.

Meanwhile, back in our hotel room, things were not going well. The television remote didn't work and it took several trips by the bellboy to replace the batteries. The heat vent was blowing cold air, which required a technician with a ladder. We unpacked as he tinkered inside the ceiling opening. An hour later, he muttered something in Italian that didn't sound encouraging and left. The vent was still blowing cold air.

The management, eager to please what few American tourists they had, offered us an identical room next door. Edna and I began the resettlement process. Our new room had only two working television channels and the beds were made up European style, with a lofty duvet and no top sheets. I didn't care. The space was cozy and I was exhausted. We slept until we were awakened the next morning by a German tour guide describing the statuary below the balcony. German is not a language by which you

want to be awakened. I felt like I had been rousted out of
bed by Sergeant Schultz for a morning roll call.

Now, Edna and I have been friends for years, but
you don't know someone until you travel with her. I soon
discovered that we were totally incompatible. She wanted
the room cold enough to hang a side of beef, I wanted cozy.
I read myself to sleep, she preferred to watch television, even
in Italian. In the morning, she was a virtual symphony of
bronchial and nasal sounds—snorts, sniffs, coughs, sighs,
groans. I would later ask Harry how he managed.

"Earplugs," he said. "I forgot to tell you. You gotta have
earplugs to sleep anywhere near Edna."

By her second cup of coffee each morning, Edna was
herself. She said that to "conquer a city" we must "summarize,
prioritize, and capitalize." I wasn't sure what that meant, but
felt certain it would require a lot of walking.

Our first stop was in Piazza San Marco, which had
nearly as many pigeons per square meter as tourists. I was
flapping them away and looking like the woman in the
Alfred Hitchcock horror film *The Birds*.

Edna, whose mind is a lint trap of trivia, took up for the
pigeons.

"Pigeons are loyal and courageous," she said. "The
army gave a medal to Cher Ami, the World War I carrier
pigeon who delivered his message in spite of being critically
wounded."

"Where did you hear that?" I asked.

"I read it in the *Complete Idiot's Guide to World War I*. If you'd like to see this heroic little fella, he's on display at the Smithsonian."

Now, while I admire Edna's inquisitive mind, her judgment sometimes leaves much to be desired. For instance, she delayed our gondola ride until the last day. Without reading the guide book, I know the cardinal rule of sightseeing—especially during the off season: strike while the iron's hot. That is, when the weather is pleasant, do what you must do. Seize the moment—or as the early Romans would say, *carpe diem*.

Predictably, our last day in Venice was the chilliest of our stay. Still, Edna said we must "gondola," else what would we tell our friends back home. In keeping with the temperature plunge, the gondoliers were all wearing goose down jackets over their blue-and-white striped shirts. Their straw hats had been replaced by hoods. I, too, put on multiple layers of clothes—a thermal shirt, long-sleeved turtleneck, and sweater, topped with a light raincoat. I was swaddled about the face and neck with a six-foot-long scarf on loan from my granddaughter. I stood with my arms stiffly out from my sides like a child overdressed for sledding.

Once on the street, Edna began her search for an appropriate boatman, one who would look good in the photographs.

"No use hiring an ugly gondolier when you have a

choice," she explained, as she looked them over. She finally made a selection and began negotiating our fare.

"*Buon giorno, signor,*" she said, overpronouncing what little Italian she had been able to pick up from the phrase book.

The gentleman smiled and responded in flawless English. We learned that our oarsman's name was Giovanni and that he was a third-generation gondolier.

"Do you sing opera?" Edna asked, as if that were a condition of our employment contract for the forty-five minute ride.

"*Si,* madam. Everyone in Venice sings opera"—though he would later claim a raspy throat prevented his performance that day.

The guide books noted the trip is more memorable if you have a bit of wine as you float the narrow, back canals of the city. With a helping hand from Giovanni we lumbered aboard, bearing two glasses and a bottle of wine, in addition to our oversize purses. As we passed under a bridge—or overpass, as Edna called the arched walkways that span the canals—we greatly amused some Japanese tourists, who immediately snapped our picture. In response we lifted our glasses in a toast, causing yet more laughter from the group.

"What do you suppose they're saying?" Edna asked.

"I think a loose translation might be 'crazy Americans.'"

That evening we had our final servings of pasta and gelato, which had been a consistent part of our daily fare. Much to our surprise, we had each lost weight! It must have been the stress of travel and the miles we walked that peeled off the pounds, despite our efforts to the contrary. Edna said we had found the perfect diet: travel, eat, walk (repeat until the pounds fall away).

In an effort to duplicate our Venetian diet at home, I inquired of our svelte female cab driver, "Do you eat pasta every day?"

"*Si*, every day…all my life."

"How do you make your sauce? I want something quick and easy…an everyday recipe that an Italian family would use."

"Very easy." She began in broken English, "Cook chopped onion in olive oil. Must be extra-virgin. *Very important.*"

I was scribbling furiously on the back of an opera program that I found in my purse.

"Yes…yes, go on…"

"Pour in large can whole tomatoes that you crush with your hands. Then—*very important*—cut up fresh basil. Must be fresh. Add salt. Cook one hour."

"No sugar or garlic?" I asked.

"No. Do just as I say and you have very good sauce every day."

I have since tried her recipe and it is quite tasty. But Americans are never content to leave well enough alone, so I insist on adding a bit of sugar and some garlic.

We arrived home on one of those travel days when you fly all day and never see the sun go down. Harry was happy with his bottle of Italian wine, striped gondolier shirt, and straw hat that Edna bought for him. Good ol' Harry. He even promised to wear the outfit the next time he went bass fishing—but only if he could take the bottle of wine, too.

A Briefing on Underwear

The deliberate display of rear cleavage and/or large portions of one's underwear below the navel has set the hip-hop crowd apart from their elders and raised the hackles of the morality police.

Those saggy, baggy pants worn by teenagers were on the way out until town councils began fining the offense like parking zone violations. Citing the "moral decay" of our youth and the "poor civic image" reflected by droopy drawers, they may have inadvertently breathed new life into the rebellious fashion statement.

Our fascination with underwear is not new. It popped up in Bill Clinton's presidential race when he was asked the question, "Boxers or briefs?" (Although my teenaged-grandson would have said, "Boxers or tighty-whities?") I don't recall Clinton's answer, but it doesn't make any difference. Undoubtedly, the question was designed to put him in an uncomfortable bind—no pun intended. As far as I know, Hillary was never asked, "Bikinis, briefs, thongs, boy shorts, hip huggers, G-strings, granny panties, or commando?" Perhaps because there are so many options to consider, she escaped questioning.

The last time I wore trendy underwear was in the 1940s, when my mother bought me a set of panties, each with a different day of the week stitched on the front. The calendar-embossed undies were all the rage among students. For about a month, I felt compelled to comply with the appropriate day. After that, I wore whichever pair showed up on top of the stack in my dresser.

Even as a youngster, I noticed a generational difference in attitudes toward underwear. My grandmother never referred to her undies as panties or underpants. In midcentury, she wore a loose-legged, baggy-crotched variation that hit about midthigh. She called them drawers. It was a term used in the nineteenth century, when women wore full-legged undergarments beneath their long skirts. Many of today's well-proportioned grandmothers wear undies that dip below the belly button and hover daringly along the hipline with a sliver of fabric stretched between the legs. You can tell, because they are constantly picking at their butts, trying to retrieve the lost string.

Some teenage boys work to get just the right droop to their jeans to reveal a portion of their underwear. This is especially annoying to their elders. Recently, I was waiting in the pharmacy line at the grocery store. Teenagers were forming a line nearby to apply for summer employment. They each had their application form in hand and were waiting their turn for an interview. I noticed they were all wearing jeans and a T-shirt—standard teenage fare. Watching them interact, I wondered which would be selected for the few available jobs.

When a boy appeared at the end of the line, wearing saggy pants and exposed skivvies, I thought to myself, that kid will never make the cut. But he surprised me. Within minutes he had sized up the competition. He began hiking up his pants, stuffing in his underwear, and tightening his belt. No mother or teacher was there yelling at him. He figured it out himself. He decided that showing his underwear might not be in his best interest. I thought, *Here's a kid who is quick to catch on and adopt a new strategy when needed.* I was encouraged. This was a good sign. Besides, I didn't want to deal with a bagger who had to devote one arm to holding up his pants while packing my groceries.

Although I no longer have children at home to harass about their attire, I still feel compelled to offer some counsel, which—since I am a septuagenarian—will be roundly ignored.

Here are my new rules:

1.   Droppage should not be such that it impedes the
      normal requirements of brisk walking, or even
      running, in the event of a terrorist attack. This is
      a homeland security issue, folks.
2.   No show of cleavage is allowed unless you're a
      card-carrying member of the plumbers' union
      or a sufferer of derrière-deficiency syndrome
      (DDS).
3.   If underwear is to be displayed, it must be worn
      on the outside, over the pants. This will provide
      a colorful accessory and the elastic top will hold
      the outer pants in place, in lieu of a belt.

Other than that, my only suggestion to crotchety city councils fretting over the current outrage of our youth is to read "Underwear" by Lawrence Ferlinghetti. In his poem, Ferlinghetti makes a good case for his conclusion: "Underwear controls everything in the end."

I'm wondering if proper underwear is a global problem. Do the half-naked mothers in western New Guinea ever say to their teenage sons, "Pull up your penis gourd. You're going to embarrass the tribe when they print our pictures in *National Geographic*."

The Power of Chicken Soup

I fell yesterday—which isn't all that bad when you are six years old. You just cry, collect hugs, and run on your way. But when you're seventy-seven, your life passes before your eyes on the way to the ground. You remember how tragic a fall used to be for an old person. You would invariably break a hip, which was equivalent to a race horse breaking its leg. You were a goner.

When the elderly take a tumble, they don't try to mask their clumsiness like some runway model falling from her stilettos, so I sat there for a few minutes checking my body parts. My pride was jarred, but I was otherwise intact.

The next day, I was sitting up in bed with one leg elevated, feeling immensely sorry for myself, when the phone rang.

"What happened to you?" Edna asked breathlessly before I could even say hello.

"Oh, I'm okay," I said softly, with only a hint of sedation.

"I heard you took a tumble yesterday."

"Actually, I took a twist. My foot just landed sideways when I stepped from the curb."

"I'll be right over," she replied and hung up the phone abruptly.

Not long afterward, Edna showed up at my bedside with her famed chicken soup. She claims the smell alone has recuperative powers.

"How did you make a pot of soup so fast?" I asked, knowing that hers was an old family recipe that calls for sixteen ingredients, half of which nobody ever has on hand.

"You don't have to start with a live chicken anymore," she laughed. "Besides, I keep a batch or two in the freezer in case Harry comes down with the flu." Edna began arranging the clutter on my night table.

"Now that you're laid up for a few days, what are you doing to occupy your mind?" she asked.

"So far, I've balanced my checkbook, picked the fuzz balls off all my sweaters, and renewed correspondence with people who haven't heard from me in twenty years."

"Would you like for me to read you today's newspaper?" she asked.

"No, my eyes are working just fine. I'm overdosed on news. Just ask me a question. Anything you want to know… go ahead…test me."

Edna ignored my request. "What about a nice cup of herbal tea?" she said, as she began fluffing my pillow.

"That would result in my having to get out of bed and go to the bathroom, and that's an adventure."

Frustrated by my resistance, she assumed the medical air that friends reserve for such occasions. "Let Edna take a look at that ankle," she said sweetly, placing her glasses on the end of her nose.

"Oh, come on, you're beginning to remind me of Nurse Jane."

"Was that the mean, old gal in *One Flew Over the Cuckoo's Nest?*" she said defensively.

"No, that was Nurse Ratched—a different species. Don't you remember Nurse Jane Fuzzy-Wuzzy, the muskrat lady, who was the housekeeper for Uncle Wiggily Longears?"

"Oh yes, I always thought that was a weird relationship, him being an elderly rabbit and her a live-in muskrat. And that Sammie and Susie Littletail seemed to be of uncertain parentage. But we didn't pick on those characters back then the way we do the Teletubbies today."

"Edna, do you want to look at this foot or not?" I chided impatiently.

As she leaned over the bed with the bewildered look of a first-year med student, I grimaced. "Be gentle, don't touch anything that's Technicolor."

Edna lifted the icepack, revealing my bruised and

swollen foot. "Wow! You've got enough color here to be a model in a tattoo parlor." Tracing her finger along one of the bruised areas, she said, "How cute! This looks like a little butterfly, and in a few days, this area on the top of your foot could be a lovely orchid blossom."

"Very funny, Edna. I have no desire to be the Foot Goddess of the Month for *Miami Ink*."

"I just want you to keep your injury in perspective," she said. "In any listing of bad things that can happen to you, this has got to be at the foot of the list, so to speak."

"That's easy for you to say, standing there on your two perfectly good feet, thinking about the once-a-season linen sale at Macy's tomorrow."

"Well, I was planning to go to the sale, but if it makes you feel any better, I'll just skip it in deference to your condition."

"Now you're just trying to make me feel worse. I insist that you go to the sale."

"No, no, I'm not going," she said adamantly. "I'm just about out of sheets and towels, but I'll just wait for the spring sales…they're almost as good…I'll get by," she trailed off.

When I didn't reply, she paused for a moment. I held my breath. When Edna takes time to think, she always comes up with a dumb idea. She didn't disappoint.

"I've got it!" she said excitedly. "There's a way we can both go."

"How's that?"

"Well, you remember when Harry broke his leg a few years back? The wheelchair he used is still in the basement. I could dust it off and…"

"I don't like this idea already," I interrupted. "I'm not going to be pushed around the mall in a wheelchair."

"Why not? It's better than lying here in the bed gazing at your foot. We could prop your leg straight out and it would be a great ramrod for getting through the crowd."

"Ouch! That hurts just thinking about it."

Two bowls of soup later, I gave in. The only way Edna would go to the linen sale was for me to go with her—on wheels.

"It will be terribly crowded. Where will we park?" I asked.

"Handicapped. You know those spaces near the door that you've been passing up all these years? Now it's your turn to park there."

"But I'm just temporarily injured," I protested.

"No matter. This is going to work just fine."

As it happened, the disabled permit holders were out in force the next day, so we had to park at the far end of the lot. Harry came along to unfold the wheelchair and hoist me aboard. The icy patches underfoot only added to the drama. I was glad to be on wheels and Edna was glad to be clutching the chair handles as a "walker."

By the time we got to the store, they were all out of white sheets and she had to get some gosh-awful yellow ones that were 60 percent off. Upon our return to the lot, the sun was shining and the ice was beginning to melt. Best of all, my foot was no longer throbbing.

"Getting out was good for me," I said. "My foot feels much better."

"It was the chicken soup," Edna beamed.

Harry announced, with a twinkle in his eye, that he felt a touch of flu coming on.

"Do you, sweet cakes?" Edna cooed affectionately. "When we get home, Momma will thaw a bowl of that yummy chicken soup and you'll be better in no time."

"Go for it, Harry," I said. "She's already cured one person this week and you could be the next."

The Queen of Clean vs. the Mother of Clutter

Have you watched the television show where a team of experts goes to the home of some poor slob who can't get his/her life together and offers professional help? The slob is usually a happy-go-lucky person with a proclivity for collecting junk and a need to have it within easy reach. The individual's living room and bedroom invariably look like a landfill with a narrow pathway leading from pile to pile.

It's all too disgusting. But these sanitation psychologists boldly take on the task, which usually requires a little therapy to get the slob on board for the project. The excavation team poses such questions as: "Do you really need a collection of two thousand dolls...or ten thousand salt and pepper shakers...or a room lined with vintage beer bottles...or an iguana and three rabbits?"

Most say they do.

But these professional tormentors appeal to the person's desire for cold cash and more walking space by offering to hold a yard sale to get rid of the accumulation. The home owners resist, but always give in, though they occasionally try to sneak items off the sale tables and back into the house.

The saga ends happily with hundreds of dollars on hand for new furnishings and a makeover. The slob is overwhelmed by the transition, vows to change habits, and lives happily ever after. The only reason for watching the show is to gain a feeling of superiority. You can say to your family, "See, this place looks like an operating room compared to *that* house."

The need to accumulate strikes the best of people. I once had a neighbor who kept everything within arm's reach or at least easy walking distance. Hazel had a recliner that listed to one side, but she knew how to maneuver it to a comfy position. From her cushioned kingdom she ruled. When she spoke the dogs leaped and the cats scat.

Amazingly, she was able to locate whatever she needed. Magazines, tissues, dog biscuits, and aspirin were stuffed into an elasticized side pocket of the chair. Hazel could make change for a ten-dollar bill just by running her hand down the sides of the cushion and swooping up the loose coins. On a side table was a pink Princess telephone, an assortment of pencils, a *TV Guide*, three remotes, a Rolodex, several paperbacks, a package of Winstons, and an ashtray in the shape of Texas.

I thought of Hazel recently when I was testing a recipe that read, "Do not stir." That was her recipe for house management. She was greatly irritated if anything was stirred by an overzealous cleaning woman or family member. It was better to let everything stay where it was originally dropped rather than risk dislocation.

"Besides," she explained, "a little scruffiness makes a house a home and hides flaws in the interior design. Without clutter, a house would have no more charm than an emergency room lounge."

It's easy to criticize another's slovenliness while making excuses for your own. So, I admit that I have a few untidy habits—though I limit my disarray to my office area. Like a crime scene, it is off limits and untouchable. But I become uncomfortable when my living room, kitchen, or bedrooms take on the look of a college dorm. At the end of each day, I take a ten-minute swing through the house, gathering up newspapers, toothpicks, empty glasses, socks, and shoes. I rearrange the coffee table accumulation, fluff the pillows, stack the magazines, and go to bed with a warm feeling of accomplishment that comes from putting one's house in order.

When I do succumb to periodic bouts of untidiness, I follow Hazel's two basic rules of success.

1. You must not give a hoot what other people
    think. Be willing to take sneers and abuse from
    inferiors who don't understand your system. Do
    not give in to others who think their housing or
    office arrangement is superior to yours.

2. Distrust the Dewey Decimal System, label-
    making gadgets, color-coded files, and anything
    numbered or alphabetized that imposes someone
    else's structure on you. "A place for everything
    and everything in its place" doesn't work for you.
    You are unique and fully capable of devising your
    own organizational scheme. The question is:
    Can you find what you're looking for in ninety
    seconds or less? Hazel could.

My friend, Edna, says I am a secret clutteress (a female clutterer), hiding my guilt behind closed doors.

"Well, aren't *we* the Queen of Clean," I responded sarcastically, as she began to inspect my kitchen.

"Seriously, let's take a look at your refrigerator," she said, attempting to make her point.

"No, no!" I said, throwing my body and outstretched arms across the refrigerator door.

"Oh, come on. It can't be all that bad," she laughed as

she pried open the door. "Let's pretend that I'm part of the sanitation team on the television show, specializing in refrigerator surveillance. Let's look at the date on these salad dressings."

"This one says 1896," I said.

"That's part of the barcode," she replied. "See, here, it says April 10, 2004. Are you still using this?"

"Sure. It's got vinegar in it and that ought to kill any bacteria," I said.

"Do you really need five jars of mustard?" she asked.

"I'm a mustard aficionado; I can't resist a new blend."

"And look at these cute strawberries in their little fur coats," she said as she pulled a carton of berries from the depth of the refrigerator and dropped them down the disposal.

"I was wondering whatever happened to those berries. They were really expensive, too," I said sadly.

Rummaging further, she pronounced my celery flabby, my eggs outdated, my potatoes sprouted and ready to plant, and my last two slices of bread firm enough to serve as doorstops.

"Your refrigerator is clean," she concluded, "it's just that the contents need updating. I've got just the plan for you. Instead of eating at home so much, you need to socialize with family and friends. Dine out more often."

"How does that help?"

"Well, it makes sense, the less you're in your living area, the cleaner it stays. I learned that my freshman year in college. Clean it and leave it," she declared.

"Good idea," I said, "Now that my kitchen's clean, what do you say we go over to your house for dinner?"

I Dawdle;
Therefore, I Exist

Last year I got a Christmas letter from a charming family. In cataloging their annual happenings, the writer used the word *busy* umpteen times. As I recall, the husband was "busy" rotating the car tires…the wife was "busy" scrapbooking…the kids were "busy" winning pageants, scholarships, and athletic awards…the cat was "busy" sleeping by the fireplace…and the gerbil was "busy" pedaling his little exercise wheel.

I knew something was wrong when Grandma, a salty old gal who lived with them, was not mentioned in the busyness citations. I found the explanation scrawled across the bottom of the letter: "Grandma went to live with Jesús." I phoned my friend right away to express my condolences.

"Oh, you got it all wrong," she laughed. "I meant Grandma went to live with Jesús, our Mexican gardener."

The incident got me to thinking about busyness. Long before psychologists differentiated Type A personalities from Type B, the rest of us had figured out that we are not all cut from the same cloth. The so-called Type As are those who can drive the car and text message at the same time. They are more likely candidates for heart disease—or, at least, a car accident. To them, life is a busyness contest.

Type Bs live longer and drive their friends nuts. Being a Type A, I have concluded that dealing with a Type B is more hazardous to your health than eating a Big Mac three times a day. Watching those Bs slough through life creates enough stress to make the plaque in your arteries break off.

But in my dotage, I am beginning to mellow on this topic. I now believe that there is a bit of A and B in all of us. We need to know which to activate and when. For instance, it's okay to assume a state of extreme busyness when a salesman rings your doorbell.

"Always look as frazzled as possible when dealing with a door-to-door salesman," Edna advises. "It throws them off their game."

She told one religious huckster that she was a practicing Druid.

"I offered to show him photos of my pilgrimage to Stonehenge for our celebration of the spring equinox, but he resisted. When I told him I was building a sacrificial altar in the backyard, he beat a path to the pavement, saying he'd be back later. But he never returned. I suppose he was too busy," she said with a devilish grin.

"Shame on you, Edna. How could a good Episcopalian

like you do such a thing?" I said.

"It was a teaching moment," she said. "It's always good to expose the narrow-minded to new experiences."

I've been reluctant to admit it to Edna, but since my retirement, I have become a bit B-ish myself. You might call me a dawdler. I now enjoy dawdling. I dawdle over breakfast, drinking a second cup of coffee and sometimes reading the previous day's newspaper to make sure that no one I know has died, been mugged, or moved out of town. (Being B-ish doesn't mean you have to be boring or ill-informed.)

Instead of taking a shower, I stretch out in my Jacuzzi, where I can dawdle all the more, steeped in an exotic blend of spices laced with a scent of lavender. I emerge prune-skinned, but refreshed.

I dawdle at bedtime. There was time when I would toss my clothes on the floor, jump under the covers, turn off the light, and be in Snoozeville within three minutes. No more. I approach bedtime with tactical precision. I lay out my clothes for the next day, fret over my schedule for the week, floss my teeth and cleanse my pores, pull the blinds, measure out my medications, slake my dry areas in lotion, check the heat register, make sure the front door is locked, gather up some bedside reading, put my iPhone in the recharger, water the plants, check the weather forecast, and set the clock and the burglar alarm. Once in bed, I get out at least twice because I've neglected to do one or more of the above.

I also dawdle at my office, paying more attention to the mail than I once would have. Just recently I read a four-page letter from the American Association of Retired People and the fine print on an offer of a prepaid funeral plan. I even toyed with getting each of my grandkids a commemorative set of coins from the Franklin Mint.

I have been on the lookout for other dawdlers. I was buying some tomatoes from an Amish fellow at the street market this summer. He had taken dawdling to the commercial level. He buffed my tomatoes with his sleeve, gave me a history of the variety I was buying, weighed them carefully, painstakingly calculated the cost on the back of a paper bag, counted out my change to the penny, and took my e-mail address so he could keep me posted on his other offerings. All this while a long line of impatient shoppers gritted their teeth.

I have another fine dawdler in my teenaged grandson. When I tell him it is bedtime, he responds with such dawdlisms as: "Just let me finish this chapter" or "This show is nearly over" or "I'll be off the phone in just a minute, I promise."

I learn so much from him.

When I told Edna of my dawdlistic behavior, she was shocked.

"Get a hold of yourself, woman," she declared. "Next thing you know, you'll be signing up to be a Walmart greeter."

"Hmmm," I said, "You may be on to something there... how much do they pay?"

A Sock in the Hand Is Worth Two in the Washer

I live alone, so it doesn't make sense that someone is making off with my socks. I have no kids or pets around, yet my socks still stray. Ever since the days of Mrs. Murphy, items of clothing have had a way of turning up in the chowder and other unlikely places. The poor housewife had to stand the humiliation of both the loss as well as the awkward discovery. Times have not changed.

Back when I managed a household of seven, which meant a minimum of fourteen socks a day to find their way to the washer and back, there was a lot of room for error. I learned that if you want to keep your self-esteem, the important thing is to shun the guilt for any lost item of laundry. I recall one morning being awakened by a child dangling a sock in my face.

"Do you know where my other sock is?" he asked tauntingly.

Opening one eye, I rolled over and said, "I give up, where is it?"

"Don't be funny, Mom, just answer the question."

"Oh," I said blurry-eyed. "I know what we're doing. We're playing Trivial Pursuit and I must have fallen asleep. Sorry, but I'll have to pass on that question. Give me one from the 1940s category."

Even today, I find missing socks, like UFOs, are an unexplained mystery. For years I have been suspicious of washers and dryers with their insatiable appetite for footwear. I have heard so many explanations. Some say socks get bored of their partner and wander off. Or they orbit the earth in a netherland where all good socks float, waiting to be reunited in the hereafter.

My curiosity got the best of me once as I watched the repair man delve the insides of my dryer. I expected to get a glimpse of spare sock heaven. To my surprise, there were no socks or pieces of socks anywhere. Only dust bunnies hopping about.

It didn't take me long to realize I was on to something big! I knew one of two things had to be true: either socks are reincarnated as dust bunnies or socks are lost before they get to the laundry room.

Simply stated, socks that go into the washer in pairs

come out in pairs; those that go in as loners come out that way. The culprit is not the machinery, but the human who misplaces his/her socks before they ever get to the laundry room. When I revealed my discovery to my family, they ridiculed me for proposing such an absurdity. But I remained strong, feeling time would prove me right. After that, I had no more guilt. I dismissed the charges of family members hovering over my bed with trumped-up sock charges.

Innovation has brought help to sockophobic women looking to ease the burden of housewifery. On the Internet you can buy Sock Clips with gripper teeth that ensure each set of socks remains one pair, indivisible. A set of thirty-two clips is only $14.95. When attached, they keep socks united throughout the washing and drying cycles and remain clipped together when tossed into a drawer. My friend Edna ordered a set. She said after two weeks, she is down to just seventeen clips. Now she is chasing both socks and clips.

I told her of the day, years ago, when I took command of the footwear situation in my house. I gathered every sock from all sources and laid them out on the bed. With the zeal of a village matchmaker, I reunited fifteen pairs and was brave enough to throw away the remainder.

Such a simple task, but, oh, the joy! It was worth it to overhear one of the kids say, "Gee, look at all these great new socks Mom bought for us."

Flush with success in reuniting socks, I took on

missing lids. At first, I thought my Tupperware lids were disintegrating in the dishwasher from high water temperatures or an interaction with the dishwashing soap. Then one day I was cleaning out the kids' room and found a half-dozen lids in their toy box. My son explained. "You weren't using them, so we turned them into Frisbees."

"Don't tell me, you've been making sock puppets, too."

"Only with the dirty socks," he replied.

Mall Talk

Dressed in our velour jogging suits with matching tennies, Edna, Verna, and I were on our third lap around the mall. We are not part of the bouncy, elbow-pumping power walkers. We are strollers. And for good reason. Between us, we have one hip and two knee replacements, one pacemaker, three bad backs, and a set of weak ankles. We take an occasional time-out. Today we stopped to watch a store clerk dressing a fashion mannequin in a new spring outfit.

"I saw in the *New York Times* that gray is the color we're supposed to wear this year," Edna announced as the clerk stretched a garment over the perfectly proportioned form.

"I think the fashion world is just reflecting on the bad economy," Verna noted. "Gray is associated with bleakness."

"I don't see it that way," I said. "I feel like gray is soft, comforting, and soothing. Just what we need in uncertain times."

"You sure don't feel that way about gray hair," Edna chided.

I hate it when I set myself up for one of Edna's "gotcha" comebacks. I was struggling to defend my position, when Verna stopped in her tracks, slapped her thigh, and muttered, "Doggone it!" That's about as profane as Verna ever gets, so I knew something was troubling her.

"What's wrong?" Edna asked.

"I forgot to move the clothes from the washer to the dryer this morning," she said.

"Don't worry," I said, "they'll still be there waiting for you, stiff as cardboard."

"But Al is out of clean underwear and I told him he could find some in the dryer," she replied.

"Rather than wear stiff, wet underwear, I bet he figures out how to make the transfer and turn on the dryer," I said.

Edna interrupted. "Verna, don't say that you 'forgot.'"

"Why, is it bad English?"

"No, it's just that women of a certain age should never admit that their memory is faulty. If you don't remember something when you're sixteen, nobody takes notice. But when you're sixty or seventy-ish, your friends and relatives start adding up those 'forgets,' and pretty soon you're off to Happy Acres Retirement Home."

"You have a point," Verna said. "So what should I say? I can't think of any way to explain to Al that his shorts are wet when he was expecting a dryer load of nice warm underwear."

"Maybe you have too much on your mind," Edna added. "You know we have tens of thousands of thoughts every day. I have to think about more than one thing at a time so I can get them all in before bedtime."

"Really?" Verna said. "I don't have more than a dozen thoughts all day and some of those are not worth mentioning."

"You're not counting all your thoughts. You have more thoughts than you think." I shook my head, not believing I had just uttered such an asinine statement.

Edna butted in. "Let me help here. Verna, when you brush your teeth in the morning, what do you think about?"

"Nothing."

"That can't be." Edna declared, "We all think about something. Take the other morning, for instance, when I was brushing my teeth. I thought to myself, I need a new toothbrush. I need to see my dentist, too. The light is awfully dim in here. One of those overhead bulbs is out. Why didn't Harry notice that? This toothpaste is nearly gone. Why does he squeeze the tube in the middle? Better put toothpaste on the store list. Bananas, too. Why hasn't my daughter called this week? My teeth are beginning to look discolored. I didn't see that wrinkle last night. Maybe it's just a sleep mark. I need a facelift. I also need carrots for the stew tonight. I wonder if eating blueberries is staining my teeth or is it the coffee. That's enough brushing. I don't want to wear the enamel off. What is Harry yelling about now? Oh, my heavens, it's eight thirty.

"You see what I mean. We have random thoughts all the time. They don't have to be scientific formulas or Greek philosophy. If you would like to share the inner workings of your brain, you could tweet your thoughts," she said.

"What are you talking about?"

"On Twitter I could instantly record all those thoughts that I had while brushing my teeth and others with too much time on their hands would ponder their meaning."

Verna looked perplexed. "Why would anybody over fifteen want to do that?"

"Come on, you two. The doughnut shop is open now. A dose of carbs should add to our thighs, if not our thoughts."

As we nestled into the booth, an already bored waitress appeared to take our order.

"I want a doughnut. Something in gray," Edna teased. "You know gray is in this year."

The waitress sighed and said, "Ma'am, all we got is powdered sugar, glazed, or cake, with or without sprinkles. And none of them's gray."

"What about the cranberry doughnuts? Don't they take on a grayish color sometimes if the batter is overmixed?"

I got up and headed for the restroom and Verna followed me.

The last I heard was the waitress patiently agreeing that

the cranberry doughnuts might have a grayish cast. By the time we got back, Edna had nearly finished her cranberry doughnut, saving only enough to show us she was right about the color.

Just then Verna's cell phone went off with the volume of an alarm system. We jumped; those at tables around us jumped.

"Oh, my lands, my cell phone's ringing!" she exclaimed.

"Okay, so answer it before the security guards come running in here," Edna said.

"But it never rings. I've carried it for years just in case of an emergency."

"Hurry up, it must be important," I said.

Verna reached into her jacket pocket nervously and fished out her hefty, old, no-frills Nokia, the kind you can't crack on concrete or drown in the bathtub.

"Hello," she said, with a slight tremble in her voice. Then with a sigh of relief, she whispered to us, "It's just Al."

"Sure, I'll pick it up for you." She added, "Oh, and I'm sorry about the underwear. You, what? Really? Well, I'll be home in a little while."

Verna punched several buttons before she found what she called the hang-up button. "I never know how to turn off these gadgets. Nothing is labeled OFF anymore."

"We don't care about that. What did Al want? Is something wrong at home?" I asked.

"Oh, no, everything's fine. He just wanted me to pick up his prescription at the drugstore. But this was weird. He found his underwear in the *dryer*! That means I didn't forget to transfer the wash."

No one said anything. Not even Edna. Verna was apparently having some mental acuity problems at home that we had not observed.

That afternoon Verna called.

"I'm okay," she said with a sound of relief in her voice. "Al confessed that he was playing a trick on me. You know this is April Fool's Day. He thought it would be funny to make me think I transferred the wash, when I really forgot to do it."

"I have a baseball bat if you need it." I said.

"No, the joke's on him," she laughed. "I told Al, 'The next time your damn underwear gets dirty, you can wash it yourself.'"

For Verna, that's stern stuff.

"What Do You Want for Your Birthday?"

I'm thinking my adult kids are slow learners. Year after year they make the same mistake. They ask me what I want for my birthday or what I want for Christmas, rather than running off to the mall the day before and getting whatever is on sale at the time. I don't make gift selection easy for them. One year, when they posed the usual what-do-you-want question, I replied: a windmill.

"Oh, have you found a wrought-iron piece at the garden shop?" one asked. "Or a cute ceramic for your knickknack shelf?"

"No, I'm talking about an honest-to-goodness windmill. One of those that sits in a farm field and goes *whirrrr*," I said, flailing my arms.

Well, I didn't get my windmill that year. It took a while for the impact of the request to sink in. But a few years later, I did. Persistence and guilt pay off when it comes to dealing with your adult children. One Christmas, my windmill arrived in the back of a farm truck—all fifty-some pieces. It was gorgeous. It took months to assemble, but I now have a spinning windmill to amuse me during weekend visits to my farm. Some things are worth the wait. (Come to think of it, that's the same thing Edna says as she downs a slice of chocolate cake—"Some things are worth the *weight*.")

Occasionally, I receive a gift that my family thinks I need or should want. They once gave me a personal trainer for Christmas. All I had to do was show up at the gym and put my body in the hands of a 110-pound woman who had trained with the CIA at Guantanamo—or so I thought. As it turned out, this was the gift that kept on giving. I took to having a paid torturess and have stuck with her for the last seven years. I go twice a week to pump iron—or pump rust, as we septuagenarians like to jest. My body doesn't look all that much better, but I can wield ten-pound weights like baton sticks and have developed a relationship with a StairMaster and a leg-press machine.

One Fourth of July weekend, many years ago, I asked for the dream gift of every serious gardener: a truckload of dried manure. All my family had to do was shovel it from a nearby barn onto a truck and unload it in my garden. Like Ma Barker, I would prepare the meal while the boys made the haul. Clearly, they were putting more of themselves into this gift than they intended, but it was such a lovely present.

By the following year, "The Fourth of July Manure Haul"—as it came to be known—was on its way to being a tradition. That year I asked for a load of wood chips for the flowerbeds; another year it was large rocks from the nearby creek bed. Whatever drudgery we undertook that required full family participation, we referred to as "The Fourth of July Manure Haul" and I looked forward to it more than I did Mother's Day. It always involved some miserable job that made you proud to be part of an American family.

When the Fourth of July rolled around last year, I asked my youngest son what he was doing over the holiday weekend. He said that he and his wife were cleaning out their basement. My eyes welled up. God bless him; he was keeping the family tradition.

It was on my seventy-fifth birthday that I played on all the heartstrings.

"This is the beginning of my fourth quarter," I told Edna, using a football analogy. "I want to do something significant."

"And what might that be for a woman who has been first lady of Missouri, a U.S. senator, and a published writer?"

"I want to see something older than I am."

"If that's all you want to do, just come down to the senior center and hang out for a few hours."

"No, I'm talking about serious antiquities like the pyramids of Egypt."

Edna got a distant look in her eye and I could tell she

was contemplating something splendid. "I see an excursion down the Nile," she said with an ethereal lilt to her voice. "You are being pampered with exotic drinks and bonbons while turbaned eunuchs stir gentle breezes with large, hand-woven fans. *Ohhh…it's so you! I love it!*"

"How can you say that? You know I'm miserable if I don't have enough to do."

"Oh, you can keep busy learning hieroglyphics or riding a camel." Grabbing her laptop computer, she began to Google the dream trip. "I found it!" she said excitedly a few minutes later.

"Here's a ten-day excursion down the Nile on an intimate sternwheeler with air-conditioning (forget the eunuchs), a library, a gracious crew, and several Egyptologists. This trip has your name written all over it," Edna chirruped.

"Only if my kids want to take out a second mortgage on their houses," I said. "Take a look at these prices. I'm thinking if I ask for this trip, the 'Fourth of July Manure Haul' will begin to look like a much better option."

"This is your big seventy-fifth birthday," Edna cooed. "Ask for both."

As Time Goes By

Being septuagenarians, Edna and I have collected more memories than Father Time. To amuse me during my recovery from hip replacement surgery, we made a list of all the things we miss from the good old days. (Understandably, hips that work headed my list.)

We composed another list of things that we didn't miss at all. Then there were the things upon which we couldn't agree or we had mixed emotions. Rather than leave those out, we just made another list. Here are the results of our limp down Memory Lane.

THINGS EDNA AND I MISS

1. Thumping watermelons, then asking the seller to plug the melon for a taste test
2. Milk delivered to the door in glass bottles by a milkman in a visored cap and white uniform
3. Large, ornate cash registers in small shops

4. Squeaky metal gliders on screened porches
5. Four-digit phone numbers with a word prefix, such as FRanklin 2408 or EMerson 2345
6. Lace curtains, but not the wood-framed stretchers needed for drying them
7. Crew cuts and white bucks
8. Burma-Shave roadway signs, with jingles such as: "She put a bullet thru his hat. / But he's had closer shaves than that. / Burma-Shave"
9. Underwear and jeans that fit the waistline. A waistline itself.
10. Bacon drippings kept in a grease container sitting near the kitchen stove
11. The scissor grinder man—his neighborhood visits heralded by a handbell
12. Wide-brimmed hats with feathers and mesh veils worn with white gloves
13. Croquet in the backyard on Sunday afternoons
14. The audible gasp in theaters when Rhett Butler said, "Frankly, my dear, I don't give a damn."
15. Recipes laced with sour cream, Velveeta, a stick of butter, and/or cream of mushroom soup
16. Devices with simple ON and OFF buttons that were large, colorful, and easily located
17. The scent of gardenias in a prom corsage

18. Walter Cronkite
19. Orange TruAde
20. Starting the school year with a new book bag, pencil box, and Big Chief pad
21. Kate Smith singing "God Bless America"
22. Groucho Marx, Red Skelton, Gracie Allen, and Fibber McGee
23. Kids perfectly entertained by jump rope, yo-yos, stoop ball, hopscotch, marbles, mumblety-peg, and dime comic books
24. Chalk rocks that can write on concrete pavement
25. Tourist homes for travelers
26. *The Shadow*, "because who knows what evil lurks in the heart of man—the Shadow knows"
27. Bugs Bunny cartoons, a Tom Mix western serial, and the World Cavalcade of News, all shown before the Saturday matinee movie
28. Knickers on little boys, pinafores on little girls
29. *Life* magazine
30. "Kilroy Was Here"—everywhere!
31. Oilcloth-covered kitchen tables in a checkered or floral pattern (some cracking or flaking allowed)
32. A uniformed professional elevator operator announcing the floors and opening the doors by hand

33. A rabbit fur muff that hung from a ribbon around the neck to keep little hands warm
34. Eating Dots, Jujubes, Crackerjacks, Wax Bottles, and Necco Wafers at the movies
35. Dish towels made from colorful feed sacks
36. Sneaking a read from *Forever Amber* or *True Confessions* magazine
37. A snowball hand shaved from a twenty-pound block of ice and doused with a syrupy grape flavor
38. Morning newspapers
39. Five-cent Popsicles from the Good Humor man
40. A hand whisk broom for sweeping fabric car upholstery
41. Those small 45-rpm records
42. Colorful aluminum water tumblers
43. Twenty-five-cent movie matinees on Saturday afternoon
44. A time when the only household item needing batteries was the flashlight
45. Cap guns and Red Ryder BB rifles
46. Captain Midnight secret decoder badge available with a label from a jar of Ovaltine, "the food drink for rocket power"
47. The 1940s, with its fifteen-cent-a-gallon gasoline, penny postcards, and $1,400 cars

THINGS EDNA AND I DON'T MISS AT ALL

1. Waiting to finish a roll of film before taking it to the drugstore to be developed—yet another wait
2. Using carbon paper to make copies and whiteout to make corrections
3. Changing a typewriter ribbon
4. Shag carpet in knotty-pine rec rooms
5. A washing machine on wheels, with an attached wringer
6. The television test pattern and accompanying ear-piercing sound
7. Garter belts, Playtex girdles, dickeys, and cheap rubber falsies
8. Wind-up watches and clocks
9. Hair-removal products that smelled like rotten eggs
10. Lampshades with the cellophane wrappers left on and chairs with crocheted arm scarves that kept falling off
11. Small tabletop electric fans in every room during a heat wave
12. Segregated restrooms, schools, churches, beaches, theaters, and water fountains
13. Typewriter erasers with a brush attached
14. Candy cigarettes, bubble gum cigars, and wax lips
15. Portable typewriters that weighed twenty pounds

16. Chain letters predicting doom for those who didn't pass them on
17. Bed pillows stuffed with chopped chicken feathers
18. Decorative wax fruit
19. Bulky mouton coats made from sheepskin and dyed to look like beaver or seal
20. Pin curls, pompadours, and permanent wave machines
21. Parakeets versed in profanity
22. Heavy, removable storm windows
23. Gregg shorthand and a job called stenographer
24. Diaper pails
25. One small bathroom per house, located on the second floor
26. Split skirts, jumpers, and lace gloves
27. Nylon hose with the seams down the back that were impossible to keep straight
28. Snowsuits with matching leggings and cap
29. Blue one-piece gym suits with name stitched over pocket
30. Before the day of antibiotics, Vicks VapoRub, the best remedy for sore throats, stuffy noses, and chest congestion
31. Saddle oxfords that required white shoe polish every day

THINGS UPON WHICH EDNA AND I
DISAGREE OR HAVE MIXED EMOTIONS

1.   Handkerchiefs with crocheted edges, starched and pressed
2.   Charm bracelets
3.   Cadillac fins
4.   Octagon soap, Duz laundry powder, and Lifebuoy bath bar
5.   Slipcovered furniture and cellophane-covered lampshades
6.   Ed Sullivan, Shirley Temple, Charlie McCarthy
7.   An ice-water bottle in every refrigerator
8.   Howard Johnson's butter-fried hot dogs on a top-split bun
9.   Licking and sticking S&H green trading stamps into books
10. Rhinestone jewelry

The Airport Patdown

Had we captured Osama bin Laden alive, we should have turned him loose in an airport security line and let the stocking-footed, dejeweled, and ungelled passengers mete out their vengeance.

Airport security began innocently enough with passenger screening. Then came the patdowns and the confiscation of sharp objects, followed by shoe removal and the ban on gels and liquids. My frustration comes as one who gets the TSA massage at each terminal, a procedure that stems from having a pacemaker and a hip replacement. Typically, I identify my condition and am escorted through a separate gate, where I wait for a female masseuse to appear. She is steely-eyed and pear-shaped. I am nonchalant and pear-shaped. On this day, her name is Finnegan. She flexes her latex-covered fingers as she prepares to palm and poke my body. I know her friends must call her "Fingers"— "Fingers" Finnegan; how could they resist?

"Would you like a private screening?" she asks professionally. I start to reply, "No, honey, I just want to get on the plane." I don't want to see how much more time I can spend with a stranger dumb enough to think the bulge around my waist comes from carrying dynamite sticks.

"Fingers" asks me to assume the scarecrow position so she can review my body for armaments. I stand there, arms outstretched, staring blankly into space, my bare feet within the yellow foot-shaped outline on the floor. Her search uncovers a paper clip, a throat lozenge, and a used Kleenex. She returns them to me and bids me good day. I always feel safer after my patdown, knowing that I am no threat to my fellow passengers.

At some airports in the United States, passengers can select between the patdown and the security scan. The scanning device, much like Superman's eyes, can see through passenger's clothing and reveal details of the body underneath. Just imagine two elderly, globetrotting women about to be x-rayed. One turns to the other and whispers softly, "Myrtle, be sure to stand up straight and hold your stomach in. You never know who's looking." How true. Supposedly, the photo of your buck-naked body is reviewed in another location and erased within minutes after it is "diagnosed" by "professionals" who, we might assume, work without pay.

We'll know how professional they are when we return to the airport after a Christmas trip only to hear the friendly security photographer quip, "Looks like we put on a few pounds around the posterior since we were here last."

The TSA needs to take a new approach. Our current techniques were designed for the first generation of terrorists and times have changed.

As any airline passenger knows, manufacturing explosives from water, gels, and lotions is a chemistry project doomed to failure. The new, downsized cabins make it impossible to do anything that requires more agility than opening a bag of pretzels. Imagine a suicide bomber with his mind on the virgins in the hereafter, trying to produce a bomb atop a seat tray. A sudden bout of turbulence or bump from the oversized guy in the next seat, and an entire terrorist plot is foiled.

Shoe bombs are impractical, too, because passengers can no longer reach their feet without moving into the aisle. At this point the terrorist is in grave danger. He must beware of passengers. These poor souls have suffered enough indignities just getting onboard. They are edgy. One false move from a suspicious-acting traveler and they'll be on him like a duck on a June bug.

So what should we do? I am one who makes lemonade when given lemons, so I propose a solution. Follow me closely here…

When we undergo an outpatient medical procedure, we slip on one of those flimsy smocks with at least one tie missing from the backside, right? We line up awaiting our turn, feeling very vulnerable as the medical wizards perform their magic. Then we re-dress and go on our way.

Why can't airports do something similar? Let them provide dressing rooms where we can stash our clothing like Clark Kent and change into our In-Flight Garments (INFIG) for travel. The one-size-fits-all smock would resemble a belted Hawaiian muumuu and come in a variety of colors.

Special shades would designate first-class passengers and frequent flyers or those requiring travel assistance or a vegan meal. Corporate users could add the company logo or advertising slogan. For a price, Cialis or Viacom could have their sales messages emblazoned on their INFIG. The possibilities are endless.

This security procedure is so much easier, cheaper, and less insidious than those potentially hazardous and annoying X-rays. I am so excited! Just thinking about In-Flight Garments makes me want one—or two—with matching flip-flops and travel bag, of course.

Sweet Dreams

"You gals are sound sleepers," Verna said as we hovered over our morning latte and pastry at the mall. "What's your secret?"

"I sleep the best on those days I get the most exercise," I said.

"I use my father's sleep inducer. Something he called his 'hot toddy,'" Edna said. "He drank a mixture of warm milk, with a drop of vanilla extract and a teaspoon of honey, about a half hour before bedtime and slept like a baby."

"Come to think of it, my grandmother did that, too, only she dunked graham crackers in the warm milk," Verna said.

"Hmmm…yummy," I said, "My eyelids are getting heavy just thinking about it."

Now Edna can easily shift into a taunting mode when given an opening, which I had clearly provided.

"Your eyelids are getting heavy because you're too much of a chicken to get an eye lift," she said fluttering her surgically enhanced eyelids.

"I've told you before, I'm not into elective pain and bruising," I reminded her. "Besides, I don't see anything wrong with my eyes."

"Of course, you don't. If you had your cataracts removed, you could see for yourself," Edna shot back.

Fearing that I might smack Edna upside the head with a Danish, Verna began to redirect the conversation.

"Time-out, you two," she said, making a T sign with her fingers. "The question on the floor is not the condition of Jean's eyes—though they *do* warrant further discussion—it's about my sleep problem."

"Oh, all right," Edna said, "what's your trouble?"

"Well, I've been having this recurring dream…"

Edna lowered her eyeglasses on her nose, the better to diagnose Verna's problem, and asked, "Have you been eating anything spicy, exotic, or caffeinated within three hours of bedtime?"

"No, I'm eating as I always do."

"You're not fanaticizing again about being Cary Grant's leading lady, are you?" she asked.

"No, this one's even weirder than that. In my dream I'm getting a telephone call that I can't hear because I'm not wearing my hearing aids."

"Of course not, you're asleep," Edna said.

"Right. Because I can't hear, I don't know who the caller is or what he wants to tell me, so I keep asking him to repeat the message."

Edna laughed. "So what's new? You do that when you're awake."

"But what if I'm missing something important that I should be hearing?"

"You mean like a garbled voicemail left on your cell phone?" Edna asked.

"Exactly. Could I be getting, say, an extraterrestrial message during my dream?"

"You're right," I said teasingly. "You could be the homework assignment for some teenage space alien, whose school day coincides with your bedtime. Or maybe a mischievous robot from another planet is playing a trick on you, knowing that you're easy to spook."

"I guess something like that is possible," she agreed sheepishly.

It was then that Edna introduced one of her more reasoned thoughts.

"Look, Verna," she said, "if someone from outer space wanted to contact us here on Earth, he would do better than whisper into the ear of a seventy-five-year-old woman who's half deaf and fast asleep."

"Well, I *am* a good listener," she said defensively. "Just in case, I get another dream phone call, I've started wearing my hearings aids to bed."

"How's that working for you?" Edna chuckled.

"I haven't gotten anymore phone calls, but I have a new problem. Now I can't get to sleep because I can hear Al snoring louder than ever."

I offered a solution that I thought might appeal to Verna. "I'll tell you what to do. Quit wearing the hearing aids to bed. And the next time you have a dream caller, just say, 'Sorry I missed your call. I am asleep at the moment. Please leave your name, number, and a brief message and I will get back with you as soon as possible. Thank you.' Then imagine yourself replaying the message in the morning after you're awake and amplified."

"I'll give it a try," she said.

Weeks passed and Verna never spoke of her dream caller again. Then one day I brought it up.

"Whatever happened to that teenage Martian, or whoever, that was bugging your sleep?"

"I only heard back from him once," she said, seeming reluctant to talk about it any further.

"And…?"

"It was a wrong number."

"What! *A wrong number?*

"Yeah…he was looking for Britney Spears."

You Can't Pet a Fish

Edna and I were sitting in my kitchen, munching on our first BLT sandwiches of the season, the ones that I make when the first vine-ripe tomatoes appear on my doorstep, compliments of a successful gardener. As the smell of bacon drifted through my kitchen, Edna made one of her leaps of logic.

"Whatever happened to that pet pig your niece kept in her backyard? That was one mean porker, as I remember."

"You mean, Stella, the pot-bellied pig? I think she died of a heart attack."

"I'm not surprised. She was overweight."

"I don't think overweight counts in a pig," I added. "They're supposed to be fat, as in 'fat as a pig.' Fat's normal for pigs. Without it we wouldn't have bacon and sausage or clogged arteries. But why are we talking about this? I don't understand where this conversation is going."

Edna went silent. She took a few more bites of her sandwich before she spoke again, waiting to allow a segue to her next thought.

"I'm thinking you need a pet in your condo. Something

that is nonallergenic and easy maintenance."

"Forget it. I'm not getting a pig, if that's what you're aiming at."

"No," she said. "I'm talking about a sweet, decorator pet that adds color and life to the living room."

"You mean like Harry?" I said with a laugh, referring to Edna's husband, a dear old soul, but one who spends long hours in front of the television screen.

"I am thinking of a pet that doesn't take up as much space as Harry and requires less food and cleanup," she smiled. "That table at the end of your living room would be perfect for a nice goldfish bowl."

"For heaven sakes, Edna, I'd rather have the pig. Besides, fish bowls leave an ugly water ring on the furniture."

"No problem. You could put a doily underneath it for a retro look."

"I got rid of my last doily in 1970," I said. "And besides, if I get one fish, it would look sad and lonely and I'd have to get a second one. Then, there would be baby fish. The next thing you know, I'd be buying a wall aquarium that needed cleaning twice a month by a trained professional. It would get out of hand."

"But fish don't get lonely. Insecure owners impose their feelings onto their fish. A fish is quite happy by itself. But if your guilt becomes too great, you can give it a sense of companionship by putting a mirror in the bowl."

"That's sneaky. You want me to deceive a lonesome goldfish? What kind of a pet owner do you think I am?"

"Obviously, you're no pet owner at all," she replied.

"Now, that's unfair. It's not that I haven't had my share of household pets over the years. I've had three yellow Labs, two Saint Bernards, one Newfoundland, and a…"

"I know…'and a partridge in a pear tree.'"

"No, it was a French poodle, which gave birth to several litters, each underneath my bed."

"A goldfish would solve all those annoyances."

"My problem with your idea is that you can't pet a fish. Real pets have fur or feathers. Fish, snakes, and turtles don't qualify," I said as though I knew what I was talking about.

"So, that's your definition of a pet: fur and feathers?"

"Yes, and a real pet should be able to acknowledge your presence—or be willing to—which leaves out most cats. I expect some serious tail wagging, hand licking, or at least a loving gaze from anything I provide room and board."

"But goldfish are loyal, quiet, and nondemanding—all the qualities you look for in a good friend. And, I might add, fish do acknowledge your presence."

"You're thinking of Wanda in that movie with Don Knotts," I said. "Real fish just swim in circles and go belly up if the water temperature doesn't suit them."

"You're wrong on that. When they're hungry they come to the surface, wiggle their little tails, and make a sucking sound with their mouths. You feed them and they go back to watching their underwater television screen."

By then I had had enough of Edna's opinions on pigs and fish. I let it drop and went back to frying more bacon. But I could tell Edna was not pleased with my rejection of her pet ideas. Within moments, she leaped gingerly onto another topic—or so I thought.

"By the way, have you seen Shirley's new fake fur?"

"No, is it pretty?"

"Not really. It looks like sheared hamster. You know, Jean, a hamster might be perfect for you."

"I don't want a hamster coat, not even a fake one."

"I'm talking about a hamster for your home. They're tidy and they're pettable."

"For heaven sakes, Edna, they're *rodents*! Let me put this discussion to an end," I said emphatically. "Since you're so insistent about this pet thing, I tell you what. I'll pull out my pet rock from the 1960s. It's been happily hibernating in the basement all these years. I'll paint it to resemble a fish and plop it on the table—no bowl to clean, no feedings to remember, no hair to vacuum, and no doily to slide onto the floor. How's that?"

"I know when I'm beat," she said sadly.

"Good," I replied. "How about splitting another BLT with me?"

"Better not. My cat is expecting me home for lunch."

The Handbag from Hell

I wish I could lug around my valued possessions like the ancient nomad who loved his library so much that he packed all his scrolls onto three hundred camels and trained them to walk in alphabetical order.

To cart around my possessions, I have used basically two purses—but not at the same time. I use one for cold weather and one for warm. I have cut back on my purses to spare myself the anguish of swapping my belongings from bag to bag. I know some women who think of purses as they do neck scarves to be coordinated with each outfit, but I do not have that degree of sophistication.

One day when I admired a trendy, lime-colored bag that Edna was sporting, she suggested that I might like to "color up" my handbag wardrobe.

"You need something with splash and spunk," she declared. "Nothing says dowdy quite like a Queen Elizabeth-style pocketbook, the kind you might use to beat off an intruder."

I hated to admit it, but Edna was right. My few purses were boring and not even functional. While a purse is incredibly "pursonal," it is not always friendly. Opening the zipper and peering longingly into a deep, black hole can be intimidating. I am so embarrassed when I have to stop a transaction to pursue some item that has sunk to the bottom or gone into hiding in the torn lining. I always start any search on an optimistic note. Looking into the leather abyss I say, "I know you're in there somewhere," as I make short, swimming strokes through the contents until I reach the bottom.

The next time I was in the mall, I wandered into a specialty shop, featuring handbags only. I was wearing that "I'm-just-looking" expression that temporarily holds salesclerks at bay. I picked up a booklet that explained purse selection to the serious seeker such as myself. I discovered that bags, like cars, not only have the manufacturer's name but model names, such as the Prada Trembled Blossoms Bag, the Nancy Gonzalez Crocodile Hobo, and the Michael Kors Watchband Clutch.

I read that "trying on" a purse is essential. Eyes tend to be drawn to the purse first, so you want to make sure attention is directed to the most favorable part of the anatomy. I paused to reflect on which of my parts that might be. If you are lean and lanky, you can get away with a shoulder bag, clutch, even a duffle bag, but if you are petite, you need to downsize, because proportion is everything.

I learned, too, that if you are bottom heavy, the shoulder bag should stay above the hips, and if you have a tummy, keep any extra protrusions out of the vicinity. Obviously, there was more to bag selection than just color and function.

Armed with this new information, I tried on several bags that didn't have designer labels. I found one in lime green—a crescent-shaped bag that fit snuggly under my arm. Even the price seemed to be in correct proportion.

Standing next to me was a twenty-something fellow shopper who was testing a bag that hung to her hips. Turning to her friend she said, "Does this bag make my butt look big?" Without cracking a smile, all of us in the shop assured her that it did not, except for one male shopper who picked that moment to slush Coke down the front of his shirt. Actually, I thought the low-slung purse drew attention from some of her upper-body bulges. I didn't bother to say so, as that region didn't seem to be one of her concerns.

With the endorsement of the clerk and my new purse friend, I bought the lime-colored bag, paying more than I had intended but knowing that it would meet the approval of Edna and the other fashionistas among my acquaintance.

As soon as I got home, I shoveled my belongings from my old bag into the new one. Kerplunk! Everything fell to the bottom. There was nothing but space on the top. How can all thirty-some items in my purse be on the bottom? That defies the laws of physics.

I had to fight past the bulky strap, insert my arm nearly to the elbow, and stir the bottom to find anything. The only alternative was to upchuck the entire contents onto a table, which is a desperate procedure, like an amputation for a hangnail. Clearly, I had not improved my bag situation. Instead of "trying it on," I should have "tried it out."

I decided to take this up with my friend, Nina. Actually, she's my daughter's friend, but my daughter shares friends with me. I figure this is so her friends know what she has to endure. Nina is a designer, specializing in funky sweaters. Her knits were featured in *The Matrix* and she designed several sweaters for the Clintons when they were in the White House.

Because she is the only designer I know—or have ever known or may ever know—I presented her with my problem.

She quizzed me as if she were a physician diagnosing an ailment. "What do you open your purse for most often?" she asked.

"During the hay fever season, that would be Kleenex," I replied.

"Don't you open your purse most often for your wallet and checkbook?"

"Sad but true. I do reach for those a lot," I confessed.

"Are those items color coded?" she asked

"Well, my wallet's red, but my checkbook is black."

"Black blends," she said, "You want to replace that with a color that jumps out at you."

I made note.

"Now, besides these basics, what else do you reach for most often?"

"My keys," I said without hesitation. "I'm always rummaging for my keys."

"Are they all secured in one place on a huge, colorful key ring ornament?"

"The ring could be a tad larger," I said sheepishly.

"Okay, what else?"

"Probably, my cell phone and eyeglasses," I said. "Next would be lipstick and comb."

"And is there anything you would like to carry with you that you don't?" she inquired.

"Yes, I'd like to carry a bottle of water, a can of hair spray, and a change of shoes."

She smiled, as one might when pampering some absurd request of a three-year-old.

"Well, we might not be able to do that," she said, giving me a verbal pat on the head. "But I think I can help you. What you need is a purse organizer."

"A purse organizer? Is this a person who is an expert on cleaning out purses?" I asked, thinking of the kitchen organizer, who visited my home and made a valiant but futile effort to rearrange my pots and pans.

"Oh, no, it's an item you can get on the Internet. It looks like a collapsible ammo belt, only smaller and with nifty little pockets for all the things you carry. When you change purses you just move the organizer. It costs about twenty dollars, but it may be just what you need for purse transitioning."

Then she added, "Now that you are into purses, you might be interested in attending a purse party."

"Let me guess…is that a party where you play musical chairs with purses and take home a different one than you came with? Or is it a self-help group where purse addicts reveal their buying habits and give one another tips on purse management?"

I could tell she was beginning to sympathize with my daughter's plight, but she soldiered on.

"No," she said with a sigh. "It's a group of friends who gather in one another's home and try on trendy bags that are for sale."

"Oh, you mean like a Tupperware party."

Nina wrinkled her brow in that way the younger generation does when the older generation reaches too far back in time, beyond their recorded memory. So, I explained. Back in the sixties, a pushy saleswoman would show up on your doorstep with a suitcase full of plastic containers with matching lids—everything from a lettuce crisper to nesting refrigerator bowls. She'd convince you to book a party in exchange for some cutlery or a plastic cake carrier. The attendees were usually young mothers who were thrilled to get out of the house, even if it meant playing silly games and buying bowls.

The hostess for the event would serve homemade German chocolate cake and coffee while the Tupperware lady went through her sales routine that ended up with everybody ordering ten to twelve dollars' worth of plastic that they were getting along quite well without.

"Well, it's something like that," Nina said, "except they serve wine and cheese now, which heightens the mood and ups the sales. Everyone has a great time trying on bags to see how they feel and look."

"And I bet they say to one another, 'Does this bag make my butt look big?'" I said.

"Yeah, that's what they say. How did you know that?"

It was just a guess.

Will You Do Me
a Small Favor?

I ask small favors of my kids from time to time. For instance, after walking in the woods at the farm, I ask my daughter to check me for ticks—no, not the facial variety—the pesky, little insects that attach themselves to remote parts of your body and cling there until forcibly removed.

When my kids stop by my condo, I often have a list of "honey dos" for them. Typically, LAs (Live Aloners) accumulate such lists for the hale and hearty who visit. It makes them feel welcome. The list includes anything that requires a ladder, electrical or plumbing adjustments, or the retrieval of fallen objects from confined spaces. So when my kids ask me to do some small thing for them, I am glad to return the favor.

My son called last summer with a request. "Mom, will you pick up Andrew [that's my grandson] on Saturday morning?

He's coming in after three weeks at summer camp and we won't be home until the next day."

"No problem," I said cheerfully, after all, how hard can it be to pick up a kid from camp? I've done that before. I did a MapQuest of the location and found that the pickup site was sixteen miles across town. I arrived early, but lost my advantage by parking on the wrong side of the building, foolishly thinking the arrival point for the buses would be the front entrance. I lined up in the ninety-degree sun, awaiting the magic moment when the bus doors would open and, one by one, the occupants would be returned to their rightful owners.

I quickly noticed that I was the only grandmother in line. Parents were in shorts, sandals, and skimpy tank tops, some showing chic tattoos. I was in full-length pants to mask my varicose veins and wearing orthopedic tennis shoes to even my gait. My long-sleeved shirt was to shield the harmful effects of the sun and to mask my saggy biceps. I could tell the others in line were undecided if my sunglasses were a trendy European style or just the only pair left in my glove compartment.

Standing at the door of the bus was a camp counselor with a clipboard and a Lake Ouwanagoochie logo on her cap and shirt. I noticed that parents were signing a form to receive their returning offspring and even showing an ID card. I had left all that in the car on the other side of the parking lot and was not about to return for it and lose my place in line. Or worse yet, embarrass my grandson by making him the last one off the bus.

I would have to fake it. After all, there had to be at least fifty years' difference between me and the young lady in charge. Surely I would have some advantage.

"I'm here to pick up Andrew," I said in a matter-of-fact tone.

"Sign here," she said. "If you are not his mother...." She trailed off. Something had given me away...could it have been the wrinkles, the age spots on my hands...perhaps the sunglasses or my tattooless arm.

She continued, "Were we sent a permission slip for your pickup?"

"I have no idea," I said, "I'm just following the instructions of my son, as any good mother would do."

"Well, let's see your ID."

"Look, sweetie, I just drove sixteen miles, stood in the hot sun for the last half hour, and will wash four loads of camp-dirty laundry when I get home—would anybody but a grandmother do that?"

"Well, we're supposed to have an ID before we turn over a camper," she said weakly.

"Fine, just keep him," I said and started to walk off.

"No, wait," she said quickly, "don't go away. We don't want any leftovers this year."

Sensing the table had turned, I said, "Well, I might consider taking one off your hands. How do I know you have the authority to discharge these campers?" She pointed to the Camp Ouwanagoochie logo on her shirt and held up her camp whistle.

I sighed. "Well, I guess that will have to do," I said. "I'll allow you to release Andrew."

"Thank you," she said gratefully, as she stuck her head in the bus door and hollered, "Andrew, you're going home with your grandmother."

How awkward being picked up by a fuddy-duddy grandmother, I thought. But he bounced off the bus, gave me a big hug, and together we lugged loads of ripe laundry and camp remembrances to the car.

I spent the rest of the day washing, bleaching, rebleaching and rewashing, drying, and folding all the clothes that survived the camping ordeal. A wave of nostalgia came over me. Perhaps it was the stench of clothing about to mildew. Or the smoky, lingering scent of the campfire. Or the coins, cellophane wrappers, and wood chips at the bottom of the washer. I smiled as I turned over my camper to his parents the next day. What fun it is to do a favor when it comes with a musty scent of déjà vu.

Pistol-Packin' Mama

Edna says she's thinking of buying a handgun. I have no trouble with her packing heat, but I wonder where she's going to pack it.

"Your purse barely zips up now," I said, "and it weighs a ton."

"Yes," she agreed, "it's on the heavy side—maybe six or seven pounds."

"Okay," I said, "add the gun, the cute carrying case, the instruction manual, and some ammo and you're beginning to have weight and space problems. Not to mention the extra pressure on your arthritic shoulder."

"I've thought of all that," she beamed smartly. "I'm downsizing my purse to lessen the heftiness."

I laughed. "Face it, Edna, a woman may downsize her house, her car, even her husband, but she *never* downsizes a purse. What are you getting rid of?"

"My business card case," she said proudly. "When I meet

new people, I'll just say my name more distinctly and point to my name tag."

I didn't bother to address that one. "What else?" I asked.

"My compact. The new, improved makeup stays on longer, so I don't need to touch up my face as often. And I'm getting a money clip to hold my currency, credit cards, and a few checks, so I can get rid of my wallet."

"Okay, but what about your coin purse?"

"I really don't need one. Coins can fall to the bottom of my purse. That's where they're the most comfortable. When I tilt my bag to one side, the coins will roll to the corner and I can easily retrieve what I need."

"Oh, that's clever. The coins will be at the bottom competing with the loose Lifesavers, nail file, hearing aid batteries, car keys, toothpicks, your Obama Mama button, and all those bags of Southwest Airlines' peanuts.

"Where there's a will, there's a way," she said confidently.

"You forgot to mention your cell phone," I said.

"I'm moving it into a tasteful, red holster that I can attach to my belt."

"Now, that should fool a would-be assailant. A gun in your purse and a cell phone in your holster—your tasteful, red holster, that is. He won't know whether to shoot you or text you."

"Have you ever carried a gun?" Edna asked.

"I once carried a water gun to school and got into a heap of trouble. But I own a shotgun." I explained to Edna that I had earned a marksmanship medal from the NRA and could still pluck a respectable number of clay pigeons from the sky. But I've never considered carrying a handgun. I couldn't rely on my attacker's being sluggish enough to allow me time to fumble through my purse for a gun and remember where the safety lock was located. Few muggers are that patient.

"My mother actually deterred a robbery with her handgun," Edna countered. "She was in the grocery checkout line when the fellow in front of her eased a small gun from his coat pocket and concealed it in his hand. Momma was the only one who saw the maneuver. Before you could say 'pistol-packin' mamma,' she slipped her hand into her drawstring bag and fished out her Derringer. Just as the would-be robber started to make his move, he looked over and saw that Momma had a bead on him. The two smiled at each other pleasantly, he pocketed his revolver, paid for his groceries, and left."

"What a heartwarming story," I said. "Carry your gun if you want to, Edna, but be careful. You could be the lead story on the evening news because you inadvertently placed your gun on the store counter while rummaging for change in the bottom of your purse. I don't want to read in the local paper, 'Elderly woman brandishes firearm when unable to make change at local grocery.'"

"Hmmm…you've got a point," she said. "Maybe I should keep the change purse after all."

Power Napping Made Simple

I come from a family of snoozers. They can sleep in the car, on the sofa, at a rock concert, in the afternoon or at bedtime. Every last one of them can do this. My husband was especially talented in this regard and always took the biblical day of rest to heart. Sitting in church on Sunday morning, he would join in singing the hymns and listen attentively to the announcements and Scripture reading. But when it came time for the sermon, his eyes glazed over and his chin dropped onto his chest. Gentle repose swept over him like a gift from on high.

As long as he didn't list too awkwardly or commence heavy breathing, I let him be. But there were times when I had to chuck him in the ribs with my elbow—gently at first—then more firmly when he failed to respond. He would open one eye, wrinkle his brow, and inquire indignantly, "Why are you punching me in the side?"

"Because you're sound asleep, dammit. Now sit up and pay attention."

"You shouldn't talk like that in church," he'd mutter under his breath.

"Don't lecture me about church conduct, when you're fast asleep. At least, I can repeat the last paragraph of what the preacher just said."

"So can I," he'd say, as his eyes again drifted shut.

"It's embarrassing sitting here beside you with your head bobbing up and down like a rubber ball."

"Shhh…you shouldn't be talking during the sermon."

"What do you mean, *I shouldn't be talking?*" I said through clinched teeth. "If I wasn't talking, you'd be sound asleep."

"Right," he said, with a faint smile curling his lips.

In an effort to make amends, he would sometimes take out his pen and begin taking sermon notes on the back of the bulletin. This would occupy him for the remainder of the service, but sometimes both pen and paper would slide from his lap and I'd have to go back to the elbow attacks.

Although I was once intolerant of napsters, in recent years I have become an ardent fan of the daytime snooze. I used to choose only the night hours between ten and seven for my slumber. Now I can nod off in the dentist's office, in airport terminals, and during such thrillers as *Pirates of the Caribbean.*

If done correctly, catching a few extra z's is known as power napping. Such catnappers as Thomas Edison, Napoleon, Winston Churchill, Eleanor Roosevelt, Margaret Thatcher, and Ronald Reagan made the practice a regular part of their day. When pondering a problem, Edison liked to hop onto his workbench for a brief doze. He found that when he went from daydreaming to "twilight dreaming," he could better access his great genius. Deep sleep would make him sluggish, but the shorter interludes were invigorating. To ensure he got only the right kind of shut-eye, he would hold ball bearings in each hand that would drop and awaken him if he crossed the line. After a brief interval of sleep, he would awaken refreshed and ready to invent more light fixtures.

Edna says that in the bowels of the Empire State Building there is an inner sanctum called MetroNaps.

"People stop by for a lunch-hour snooze in the sleep pods."

"Sleep pods?" I asked. "Is that just another name for a camping cot?"

"Actually, the pods are a unique creation designed especially for MetroNaps. They resemble a legless lounge chair and tilt back at an angle that holds the body in zero-gravity position. The napper's feet are elevated and there is a bubblelike shell over the head to give a cocoon feeling. Friends and employers give workers 'nap coupons' as gifts."

"How much does it cost to purchase a nap?" I asked.

"It's about fourteen dollars for twenty minutes of blissful repose. That includes a trip to the wake station, where they have lemon-scented towels and mineral water for a wakeup spritz."

Edna has picked up on the snoozing craze and is on her way to becoming an Olympic napper. She bought all the gear needed for professional snoozing: eye shades, a nap mat, a comfy pillow, a light blanket, an iPod, earplugs, and an alarm. She even tried a sleep kit called MindSpa that combines white light and pulsating sounds to help switch the brain to its theta frequency. Now she's ogling the Pzizz Energizer (a $200 package) that promises to clear the mind and dissolve mental stress with an audio track of nature sounds and lullabies.

"If you're going to nap, it needs to be done correctly," Edna intoned. "I've fallen asleep over a lot of books on napping and one of the rules is to take your siesta between two and three in the afternoon."

"I always thought it was best to doze off when you couldn't keep your eyes open any longer," I said.

"For best results, you should first have a cup of coffee or other caffeine-laced beverage. I used to drink a glass of warm milk about an hour before my nap," she said, "but I've switched to coffee."

"No way. I would never get to sleep."

"Wrong," she said. "It takes twenty to thirty minutes for caffeine to kick in, so if you drink it just before your snooze, you'll drift off and be awakened at just the right time for the ideal nap. Your mood will be elevated and your concentration improved."

I tried it and sure enough, she's right. With Edna's help, I'm trying to take my napping to the next level. Even so, there are still times when I nod off at my computer, unassisted, leaving a trail of letters across the screen to mark my dropping-off point. Edna says my naps need more structure and suggested that I read a book by Dr. William A. Anthony entitled *The Art of Napping*.

"Who's he?" I inquired.

"He's a Nappist," she said.

"Is that a religion?" I asked.

"No," she said, "but it could be."

Home Alone

One day Edna said to me, "Living alone must be sooo…" She didn't finish the sentence. She took a deep breath and started over.

"Would you ever consider living with someone?" she blurted out.

"Why? Are you considering leaving Harry after all these years?"

"No, no," she said, "you're not tracking with me. I worry about you living alone. Could you live with another person?"

"Only if they know how to work a television remote," I replied. "My teenage grandson lived with me for two weeks. His visit was a dual treat. Not only did I enjoy his company, I benefited from having an in-house technician. I never once had to think about television programming or DVD quirks. Although I must admit there were times I felt as if I had been invaded by aliens. Spare socks showed up in strange places, my refrigerator looked like an empty tomb, my coffee table was decorated with soda cans and pizza crusts, and my

IM buddy list featured such adorable names as luvmuffin, cutemaxy, scarychick, and hockeystud."

"Seriously," she said, "you must get lonely without an adult companion."

"Edna," I said, "do you realize that I get up and go to bed when I damn well please. I listen to the television as loud as I want—sometimes until after midnight. When I feel like it, I eat pizza for breakfast or cereal for dinner without a sneer from anyone. I diet—sometimes for hours—or make an outrageously sinful dessert. I decorate, clutter, rearrange, heat, and cool this place to my heart's content. Some days—when it suits me—I write all day long. If I want company, I go to the gym, call a friend or family member, or go to the office. I can get to the grocery, drugstore, coffee shop, and mall in five minutes. I'm within seven to ten minutes of most of my children and grandchildren. What is wrong with this picture?" I asked.

She was speechless.

It's not that I didn't enjoy my other lifestyles, I explained. I was an only child with all the attendant benefits. Then as a wife and mother, I was responsible for the care, feeding, laundry service, and social calendar for seven people in my household. I loved that, too. But now I'm in to a new phase. I have simplified. I live in a condo where the pool is filled and cleaned by others, the windows washed, the lawn and shrubs tended, and the units regularly sprayed and painted.

The elevator, garage, and entry are spotless and secure. I walk out...I walk in. I enjoy. When I want rural, I spend the weekend at the family farm.

I am not alone. More than 51 percent of American women live by themselves. In 2005, married couples became a minority of all American households for the first time. The average American now spends half of his/her life outside of marriage. For many women, having an apartment of their own is a rite of passage, a swing at independence, or an opportunity to learn more about themselves. When I explained that to Edna, I knew what her next question would be.

"Well, what have you learned about yourself?" she asked predictably.

"Well, last night I had my kids and their spouses to dinner at my condo. I cooked a lovely dinner. But I discovered that I am unequipped for preparing a meal for more than one. I no longer have cake pans or a family-size salad bowl. My place mats are mismatched, as are my plates, silverware, and chairs. We had to eat the peach shortcake off of saucers. For awhile I thought we would need to share drinking glasses.

"Last winter, I had to put my Christmas tree in a corner because I only have enough lights and ornaments to decorate one side. I think I have downsized one tea cup too far," I said. "I'm missing a sense of 'householdness.'"

Edna knew exactly what I meant. "What you need is a senior shower," she said.

"Is that when you add handrails and a bench to your shower stall?"

"No, no, it's like a bridal shower, but for seniors. You can select new dinnerware and linen patterns and have them listed on the Internet. Your friends shower you with gifts. In no time at all, you're ready to entertain in style."

"Edna, that sounds like one of your Ethel Mertz ideas. Just what would I do with the odds and ends I have now?"

"You can sell your mismatches on eBay or give them to the Salvation Army—if they'll take them." She paused for a moment of reflection. "There's another solution," she said thoughtfully. "You could invite your family to dinner just one couple at a time." That didn't seem like a practical way to handle birthday celebrations, not to mention holiday get-togethers.

Sensing my lack of enthusiasm, she continued with her original train of thought. "So what else have you learned?" she asked.

"I have learned that I have a crazy and wonderful friend who looks out after me and makes sure that I'm not home alone too often."

"What are friends for?" she smiled.

Health Potion No. 9

In my grade school they issued a health card on each student. One year I got a "skinny card," suggesting that I was too thin for my age (a condition that I have since rectified). The evaluation was far from scientific. A teacher sized us up much as Goldilocks did the bowls of porridge: We were skinny, overweight, or just right.

The women of my family drifted toward roundness in their adult years. But my mother couldn't wait for me to fill out. Not wanting the teacher to think ill of me—or the family—she began making me a milkshake each night with an egg in it to fatten me up. It was like eggnog, but without the kick. My body rebelled, refusing to plump before its time. Years later, Carnation Evaporated Milk would replicate my mother's concoction, add a few vitamins, and market it as a meal in a can. In retrospect, I am proud to have once earned a "skinny card." If my doctor issued one of those today, I would post it on my refrigerator door and boast of it in my Christmas letter.

Americans have always been suckers for a quick health or energy fix. In the early fifties, a product hit the market known as Hadacol, the brainchild of a Louisiana politician turned patent medicine huckster. In addition to vitamin B, the miracle elixir had a 12 percent alcohol content, which made it popular as a beverage in the dry counties of the South. Instead of taking a tablespoon, four times a day, Hadacol enthusiasts downed it by the shot glass. Mama didn't fall for this one. At $3.50 for a twenty-four-ounce, family-size bottle, she felt her homemade shakes were a lot cheaper and more nutritious.

My grandmother was a teetotaler; that is, tea was her total beverage. She drank plain ol' Lipton tea—nothing exotic—but it apparently had a remedial effect since she lived to be ninety-three. In her house, a cup of tea was essential to solving problems, soothing pain, and enduring hardship.

Today our health potions are more sophisticated, but no less costly. Energy drinks such as Red Bull and Arizona Tea give a dose of B-complex vitamins, along with a jolt of caffeine and sometimes a dash of ginseng. But my preference is something more *au natural*. It is pomegranate juice. According to a researcher friend, the juice has done marvels in preventing Alzheimer's disease in mice. Pomegranate-treated rodents can pirouette on their hind legs, clap their paws, and prance through a complex maze lickety-split.

Well, almost. Whether it will do the same for me is yet to be seen; I am still working on the pirouette. If you find straight pomegranate a little tart for your taste, you can jazz it up with orange juice or give it some fizz with the addition of sparkling water. It doesn't count if you get your pomegranate fix from ice cream with a few of the fruit chips added.

When it comes to performance enhancing elixirs, Pat Robertson may have found the secret. Although in his late seventies, the good reverend says he can leg press two thousand pounds—a Samsonian feat that even professional football players cannot match. By golly, he may be a chicken hawk, but he ain't no "chicken-legged" hawk.

Robertson's "leg up" doesn't come from improved body parts or from prayer and meditation, as you might think. The strength in his loins comes from an "age-defying protein shake" that he concocted from a few dozen ingredients, including soy, flaxseed oil, orange juice, and apple cider vinegar. Hmmm…sounds a lot like my recipe for marinating pork steaks.

I know that my wimpy leg presses will never merit a news story. Having recently undergone hip replacement surgery (arthritis related, not leg press induced), I may need to confine my pressing to the ironing board. Then again, having a titanium hip joint might actually give me a "leg up" at the local gym and a crack at the record books. I dream.

If I can conquer the pirouette and maze run, I may

have the *bona fides* to introduce my own health drink. I'm thinking, if I take the pomegranate juice and add egg, milk, alcohol, B vitamins, and ginseng, I can capture the ultimate health potion of the century—the best of Mama's kitchen, Hadacol, Pat Robertson's elixir, and modern science.

I'm cleaning out my bathtub right now to do a test batch.

The Undercover Life of a Bookie

I have hundreds of books scattered about the house. My night table is heavy laden with unfinished paperbacks, magazines, and Internet vignettes. I'm a whimsical reader— sometimes seeking information, other times wanting to be amused or intrigued by a favorite writer. Occasionally, I just need something boring enough to put me to sleep. Edna thinks my inability to finish one book before starting a half-dozen others indicates an attention deficit disorder. I argue that my reading habits reflect a guilt complex.

"What's there to feel guilty about?" she asked.

"It all goes back to my youth. My grandmother felt that reading was a luxury, something that people did to get out of work. I remember her saying, 'You'll never amount to anything if you keep your nose stuck in a book all the time.'"

Edna tried to stifle a giggle.

"Spare me your commentary on my grandmother's

prediction." I said. "My point is, when I read for hours at a time, I often think of what she said. When I do, I close the book, jump up, and take out the trash or vacuum the drapes. It makes me feel better."

Edna nodded. "I understand," she said. "Your grandmother would have remembered a time when reading and writing competed with work. Did you know that Elizabeth Barrett Browning was diagnosed as suffering from a 'brain fungus' that supposedly afflicted women who spent too much time writing poetry?"

"I'm more worried that a fungus will grow in my bedroom from having every corner stacked with books."

"Why don't you get rid of all those dust collectors?" Edna said flippantly.

"I can't do that. They're like old friends, familiar and comforting. Maybe I need more corners."

"No, what you need is a Kindle," she said with a know-it-all toss of the head.

At first, I thought she said, "You need a Kenmore." It sounded like my grandmother thinking that a new washer or dryer would cure my book addiction.

"No, it's 'KIN-dle,'" she said, moving closer to my face and mouthing the word slowly as one does for the hearing impaired, which makes you want to slap them upside the head.

"Let me guess what that might be. You're using the

word *kindle*, so maybe it has something to do with book burning."

"You might say that," she laughed. "I found out about Kindle when I was sitting next to a man on a plane recently. He was reading from a thin, metal tablet with no cords, no connections. He had just downloaded a new book from Amazon for less than ten dollars. He also had access to newspapers, magazines, and even blogs—all on this lightweight device that costs about three hundred and sixty dollars."

"That's just another generation of the e-book," I said. "It's like reading from an Etch A Sketch. You can't flip the pages or dog-ear a corner…or massage its soft, papery texture and curvaceous spine…."

"Before you get too carried away, I might point out that they've come a long way since the old Etch A Sketch screen. Kindle has an electronic page display that makes the screen look and read like real paper. You need to have an open mind about this."

"Why is that?"

"Because I'm thinking of getting you one for your birthday loaded with the unabridged version of *War and Peace*."

"That might do more to curb my reading addiction than anything my grandmother thought up. Besides, I once tried to sludge through *War and Peace*, but despaired of dealing with all those unpronounceable Russian names."

"I got you the new, twenty-first-century version that substitutes the names of Sarah Palin's children. It's a lot breezier to read now.

"Seriously, think of it this way," Edna went on. "With a Kindle, you'd spend less on books. You'd reclaim your night table and room corners. Whether you're in the bathtub or on the beach, you'd have a world of literature at your fingertips. You could even pull it out in church and no one would know if you were reading the Psalms or the *Wall Street Journal*. And, best of all, no trees would be killed to bring you another book."

At Edna's insistence, I borrowed her Kindle for a test run. I pulled up in front of the fireplace, kicked off my shoes, and started "pressing" the pages. As I often do while reading, I fell asleep. I was awakened by my own yelp. The Kindle had fallen from my hands and onto my foot, its metal edge leaving a dent on my big toe. I told Edna the next day, when I showed her the bruise.

"This would not have happened with a real book. It would have gently splayed its pages across my foot, breaking the impact."

"You're right," she said, "I guess there's some advantage to having that 'soft, papery texture and curvaceous spine' after all."

The Beauty Secrets of a Smiling Septuagenarian

Face it, my fellow septuagenarians, we have what everyone wants—longevity. The young want to become ancient of days, but without the calcification. Can't blame 'em. All of us hope to be spared the lines, wrinkles, aches, and memory loss that come with the golden years.

Comedian Phyllis Diller summed up the problem in the title of her book: *The Joys of Aging & How to Avoid Them.* Since we have not yet found the fountain of youth, the next best thing is to avoid "geezerhood" for as long as possible. Researchers tell us that to keep from looking like Mammy Yokum, we need to stay out of the sun and tanning salons, sleep well, eat right, exercise more, and not smoke.

We all have something that we do regularly that makes us feel better. For Cleopatra, queen of the Nile, it was her daily milk and honey bath. For my grandmother, it was her evening application of Noxzema—a skin cream that came in a blue jar, with an aroma that I would still recognize today. She covered her face and hands in the mixture just before bedtime. To keep it from rubbing off, she had to sleep on her back all night and wear gloves—a small price to pay for smooth skin and the many compliments that came with it.

The Japanese answer to Noxzema and Egyptian milk baths is the steaming sake soak used in the geisha houses by women wanting to keep their skin soft and radiant. The Japanese wine contains some organic acids that supposedly renew the skin by peeling away dead cells. Proponents also claim that the steam cleaning of the pores gets rid of any "evil spirits" that might be lurking just beneath the skin. Since it is unlikely that you will find anyone offering a steaming sake soak at the mall, here's Edna's recipe for a homebrew.

Fill your bathtub with hot water, while pouring in one quart of sake under the running water. Immerse yourself and soak for half an hour. Using a washcloth, steam your face and limbs. Dry off and go to bed immediately. The steam will warm the body and make for a sound sleep. The next morning, you will awaken refreshed, energized, and silky soft.

I have not tried this. The thought of pouring a full quart of sake into my bathwater and letting it flow down the drain is too distressing—and costly—for me to consider. I'm wondering whether some cheap, undrinkable wine would work just as well.

The Chinese, on the other hand, offer a splendid pastime and health remedy—the ancient foot massage. By activating special pressure points in the feet, a masseuse can relieve stress and cure various ailments. In China you can get sixty minutes of pleasurable foot therapy for two to three dollars, plus airfare. That alone sounds like it's worth a trip. Some of these foot parlors also do plastic surgery in the back room, for those wanting a cheap repair of their droopy eyelids.

Tibetan monks have a five-step program for "youthing." The first step is to spin around with outstretched arms until you're dizzy. That's not hard to do in the Himalayas where the air is thin and you're wobbly all the time anyhow. As they say, "Do not try this at home." For the cardiac set, lightheadedness is not a good sign; it could mean the battery in your pacemaker needs recharging.

My own beauty and health secrets are far less exotic and, arguably, not even working, but I stick with them nonetheless. I see my dermatologist and dentist once a year, get my annual flu shot and breast exam, put my arm in the blood pressure cuff at the grocery store, down an occasional glass of red wine to boost my HDLs, eat a handful of antioxidant-laced blueberries every day, and sip on a bottle of pomegranate juice while working a crossword puzzle to stave off mental deterioration.

Despite the advice of anti-aging advocates, science has yet to find the fountain of youth. Dr. Leonard Hayflick, professor of anatomy at the University of California, San Francisco, says the claims are "all garbage." He writes that there "are no lifestyle changes, surgical procedures, vitamins, antioxidants, hormones, or techniques of genetic engineering available today that have been demonstrated to influence the process of aging."

I find that disheartening. I was especially optimistic about a cream that promised to unwrinkle my face and turn back the hands of time. The secret ingredient was the secretions of the humble, brown garden snail. Yep, snail poop. It might work, but I worry about the side effects. I'm concerned that people would look at me and say, "Her skin is lovely, but she sure does move slow."

Everything's a trade-off.

An Evening with the Girls

Edna and I were sitting on Verna's porch one evening, when Edna picked up a copy of *National Geographic* from the end table and pointed to the natives on the front cover.

"Look at the shirts on those guys," she said.

"What about 'em?" I asked.

"They're sparkling white! How do people living in a jungle keep their clothes spotless while I get a permanent stain on a blouse every time I eat Chinese? There must be something about pounding clothes on a rock in a cold stream that Proctor & Gamble isn't telling us."

"Don't be silly," Verna said. "They probably don't eat as much Chinese carryout as we do, so their clothes stay white longer. It's all in the food you eat."

I tried to find a middle ground before we got too far around the bend.

"Perhaps they only photograph the natives who are wearing clean shirts. That's what I'd do if I were the cameraman."

About that time, Verna set out a box of red wine and some cheese balls, causing Edna to register a ten on her Richter shock scale.

"Verna, what's with the *box of wine?*" she blurted out.

"Oh, I got that at the drugstore today. It was on special and the clerk said it was really good."

"Since when did they hire a sommelier for the checkout counter?" Edna chided. "I can't believe you bought wine in a carton as if it's orange juice, for heaven's sake."

"I thought you, of all people, would approve," Verna replied. "Don't you know that changing the packaging of wine reduces greenhouse gas emissions? Because the product weighs less, it is less costly to transport. If we put all our wine in cartons we would reduce gas emissions by two million tons, the same as retiring four hundred thousand cars."

Edna was stunned. When Verna stepped out of the room, she took a sip of the wine, shook her head and whispered, "I've taken liquid cold remedies that had more body than this."

"I think you're a wine snob," I said.

"How can you say that? I just don't like the idea of wine coming from a plastic spigot."

"Well, don't say anything. It will just hurt Verna's feelings." So we drank the wine in deference to our hostess and masked its deficiencies with cheese balls.

Several glasses into the evening, Verna set out another surprise: a four by four-inch plastic cube filled with cards.

"What's that? Edible paper?" Edna teased.

"No," Verna replied, "it's a game called Table Topics that we're going to play."

"You know I'm not good at games, Verna," I said. "I think I'll just run along home."

"No one leaves until we play the game," she said, throwing her arms out like a defensive guard.

"Okay, okay. I'll play one round…or one inning…or one hand, whatever it is," I said.

"Where did you get the game? At the drugstore?" Edna asked.

"That's right, I did." Verna replied, "How did you guess?"

I was getting impatient. "Hurry up and let's get on with this, Verna. How do you play?"

"Well, each person picks a card, reads the question on it, and then we discuss the answer," she said. "To keep the pace moving, we will limit each discussion to just three minutes, so you have to be quick. I'll go first so you get the idea."

Verna pulled out a card, snickered to herself and then read: "If you were setting up a new society, what would be the role of women?"

Edna pounced on that one. "We would be the rule makers. You know the old saying, 'Those who make the rules rule.'"

"What kind of rules would you make?" I asked in an attempt to spur conversation, as I was sure the game was intended to do.

"I would have the entire population sprayed with a contraceptive solution. Then to become parents you would take the free antidote. That way only people who truly wanted children had them. It would really solve a lot of problems."

"With my luck I'd be in the shower when the contraceptive dusting plane flew over," Verna said. "Besides, I don't like this question. You pick one, Jean."

I pulled out a card and read: "If you got a tattoo, what kind would you get and where would you put it?"

I'm not into elective pain, but I played along.

"I would get something discreet…perhaps a small butterfly on top of my big toe," I said.

"Ahhh…that's cute," Verna said.

Edna sighed her disapproval and let Verna and me ramble. After a few minutes, she tried to draw a conclusion.

"You're being too rational about this. Nobody gets up in the morning and says, 'Today I'm going to get a tattoo.' You don't elect to have some guy in a leather vest with a ponytail poke needles in your skin when you're sober—only when you're drunk or in a country whose name you can't pronounce."

That was hard to argue with, so Edna grabbed a new card and read: "What was the worst hairstyle you ever had?"

"I've liked all my hairdos…at the time," Verna said.

"Honey, you looked just awful in that beehive you wore back in seventies. I've waited all this time to get up the nerve to tell you that. It's best you don't go on thinking that was a good look."

"I think I detect a little jealousy from you, Miss Edna," Verna said curtly. "I got lots of compliments on that hairstyle."

"All right, you guys, can we reminisce more gently?" I said. "Let me give this one a try. I'd say my worst hairdo was those banana curls my mother made me wear so I would look like Shirley Temple."

"Well, did you look like her?" Edna asked.

"No, I had buck teeth, blond hair, and no eyebrows. Although I think my curls were far prettier than Shirley's."

Before I could finish describing the loveliness of my naturally curly hair, Verna was waving a new card in the air. "Listen up, girls, here's one that hits close to home: 'Which of your children would you want to take care of you in your old age?'"

"All of 'em!" Edna shouted without hesitation. "To keep

me in the manner to which I want to grow accustomed, 'it will take a village,' as Hillary might say."

Verna and I agreed that taking care of Edna would require at least a joint venture, if not a village, and quickly moved on.

I pulled the next card and read, "What's a perfect age?" There was a noticeable pause in the conversation as though we were all doing a mental calculation.

I spoke first. "There is no perfect age," I said profoundly. "No one is ever happy with what age she is."

Edna frowned. "I don't know about that," she said. "Eighteen was pretty damn good."

"Think about it. You only feel that way in retrospect. I bet you wanted to be older at the time," I said.

"Well, I definitely wanted more money, fancier clothes, another job, and a better boyfriend," she declared.

Unable to determine the perfect age within the three-minute time frame, we moved onto yet another topic, this time one that we could get our teeth into—literally.

It read, "If you had to put on ten pounds, what would you eat to gain the weight?"

We lit up with delight at the thought!

"I remember when Shelley Winters supposedly put on thirty pounds for *The Poseidon Adventure* and she never looked the same again," Edna warned.

"I tell you something crazier than that," Verna added. "I read about a prisoner on death row who ordered a salad and Diet Coke for his last meal. Why in the world would anybody do that?"

"Maybe they had a bad cook at the prison," Edna suggested. "But let's get back to the question. How are we going to put on these ten pounds...and fast?"

It didn't take long to decide that gelato and mashed potatoes would be our weight-gain foods of choice, though we differed as to which flavor of the Italian ice cream we'd use to achieve the goal.

I thought we were just getting the hang of the game, until the next question caught us all off guard.

Verna could hardly contain her amusement as she read: "Tell the truth, do you pee in the shower?"

We burst into laughter. It's surprising what a dumb question and a cheap wine will do to your sense of humor.

"That's it," I said, "I'm going home."

"Me, too," Edna chimed in. "This is a disgusting game... and so is that drugstore wine you served," she shouted back at Verna as she headed out the door. "But those cheese balls were divine."

Things Happen

There's no need to fret and fume. Some things happen so commonly that they have come to be seen as universal and predictable. Below are just a few of the laws of inevitability, most of which are well known and agreed upon.

1. Unexplained sounds are noticeable only when you are alone.

2. According to the Law of Surfaces, a spilled glass of milk will cover the same area as a gallon of paint.

3. Linen—no matter how well cared for—will wrinkle. Ditto for faces.

4. A child will bond with a reptile. At some time you will share your basement (bathroom, bedroom, laundry room) with a creature that makes ET look like a pageant winner.

5. No matter how many pairs of reading glasses you buy, eventually they will all gather like conventioneers in one room.

6.   Sound emitted from televisions, radios, stereos, or rock bands practicing in the garage will always be slightly louder than you can endure and cell phone messages will always be muffled and undecipherable. This is the Law of Acoustical Predictability.

7.   Just as you begin to roll out a piecrust, mix a meat loaf, or grease the motor, the phone will ring, your nose will itch, or a small child will bleed.

8.   Any item dropped on a hard surface will roll out of reach or at least out of view.

9.   If you change checkout lanes at the grocery store, it will move slower than the one you left. You will always have at least one more item in your cart than allowed in the quick lane. The person in front of you will have ten more.

10.   According to the Law of Happenstance you are more likely to meet someone you know whenever you are at a place you'd rather not be seen accompanied by someone you don't want to be seen with.

11.   In keeping with the Law of Celebrity Encounters you will have left your camera in the car anytime you meet a notable person.

12.   When you try to get a computer, a car, or household appliance to replicate a noise or malfunction for the repairman, it will work perfectly. This Law of Inverse Indicators also explains why your ailing body, waiting in a doctor's office, will heal itself miraculously and you will be symptom free by the time of your appointment.

13.   According to the ancient and immutable Law of the Coliseum, people with the middle seats in a row will arrive late and have small bladders. This holds true at stadiums, theaters, airplanes, and church services.

14.   Red wine and white carpet are proof of the Law of Attraction.

15.   Anytime you sit down with a hot cup of coffee and a magazine, a boss, child, husband, or pet will require your immediate attention. If you are alone, a household fly will materialize out of nowhere.

16.   Leaves fall; so do children, stock markets, vases, and arches.

17.   Clutter is infectious and, if unattended, will spread throughout the house.

18.   When someone dials you by mistake, the caller will most often ask, "Who is this?" Your best reply: "I give up. Who is it?"

19. Cookie jar lids are always cracked.

20. A knife so dull it will not cut warm butter will lay open a wound in your hand requiring four stitches.

21. You will always pull the wrong drapery cord first.

22. If you go back to check on the iron, it will be off.

23. Despite the amount of water used in a pan, carrots will burn the minute your back is turned.

24. Cleaning women will not find cobwebs, guests will.

25. Cookies brown on the bottom before they do on the top. This is Nestlé's Law of Thermodynamics.

26. You will find lost earrings (or socks or gloves) only after you have thrown away the remaining one. This is known as the Rule of Pairs.

27. As soon as you find a bra that fits perfectly, it will be discontinued.

28. There is always one annoying relative at the family reunion, funeral, or Thanksgiving dinner. Be consoled by God's response to Abraham when the ancient patriarch complained of a disagreeable guest: "I put up with him all the time, can't you put up with him for just a day?"

29. You will always be the one to change the toilet paper roll.

30.   The chance that your tickets are for seats
       adjacent to an icy air-conditioning outlet, next to
       the megawatt speaker system, or behind the lady
       with the tall hair increases with the price of the
       ticket or the significance of the event.

Yes, things happen. Or as the French would say with a
shrug of the shoulders, "*C'est la vie.*"

The 1950s Wedding

I got a wedding invitation recently—I think it was a wedding invitation. You never know anymore. Some of them look like a flier for a half-price sale at the mall. Emily Post must be pounding the lid of her coffin at what passes for propriety these days.

There was a time when formal invitations included a tissue paper insert and a packet of cards embellished with raised or engraved print. (You could always tell because engraving left an impression on the back of the card stock.)

Invitations are more practical today, but no less costly. A neighbor told me about a wedding announcement from one frugal couple that included an invitation to their baby shower in the same envelope.

"It's not the 1950s anymore," Edna reminded me. "You don't have to do everything by the book as we did. Looking back, don't you wish you had been more flamboyant?"

"Actually, I thought I was being wildly flamboyant when my bridesmaids wore pastel gowns with straps narrow enough to require a tulle shawl to comply with the church dress code."

"Even though you were married on the East Coast and I was married in the Midwest, I bet our weddings were nearly identical," Edna said. "You were married in a forty-five-minute ceremony by a minister in a non-air-conditioned church in June, right?"

"That's right."

"And you walked down the aisle as an organist played 'Here Comes the Bride.' The three songs performed at your nuptials were 'I Love You Truly,' 'Because,' and 'The Lord's Prayer.'"

"How did you know that?" I asked.

"No bride of the fifties would have done otherwise. You undoubtedly had a reception in the church basement, where they served Baptist punch and a cake topped with two plastic wedding figures."

"Wrong," I countered. "The wedding reception was in the backyard of my parents' house, where the temperature soared over ninety degrees. The cake did a slow meltdown, as did the guests. It was memorable."

"I bet your kids' weddings were nothing like that."

"The two that got married in the twenty-first century strained convention," I said.

"Strained convention? What does that mean?"

"It means traditionalists would have been aghast. One

got married in front of a huge rock outcropping at our farm. They called it an 'ancient altar.' The other spent months cleaning out our hundred-year-old barn just to have the reception dinner and dance there."

"Was that the wedding where it rained and turned the barnyard into a swamp?"

"That's the one."

"Well, you know what they say: 'When it rains on your wedding day, it is God crying tears of joy.'"

"In that case, this was one happy deity."

"I went to a wedding once where they put tattoos on the guests," Edna said.

"Just how drunk did you have to be to go along with that?"

"Not at all. It was the wedding of a Middle Eastern couple and they did these wonderful henna drawings on your hands and arms. They fade away in a few weeks, and toward the end you look like you have a skin disease.

"Another time, I went to a Renaissance wedding where the participants and guests wore costumes. It had the feel of a high school operetta. People loved it."

"I'm thinking it would be fun if someone had a 1950s wedding," I said. "Since those of the current generation have never seen one, they might find it quaint."

Edna laughed. "Maybe you should mention that to your grandkids."

"Nope, not gonna do it. I'm out of the wedding advisory business. I don't even want to be a wedding planner emeritus. I know my role: it's to buy a new outfit, keep my mouth shut, dance with the groom, and gush over the bride."

"Let me guess: the hardest part is keeping your mouth shut," Edna said.

"It runs a close second to dancing a polka with an arthritic knee."

Can I Start a Dressing Room for You?

I have a bland wardrobe of mostly solid colors. I think it comes from having served in the U.S. Senate. You just didn't show up on the floor of that august body in a wild floral or multicolored plaid—though some of the men get flashy with their tie patterns. Senator Rick Santorum had a Pepto-Bismol pink tie that looked like an anatomical diagram of the medicine's route to the stomach. When he was feeling tough, Senator Ted Stevens wore his Incredible Hulk tie—probably a Father's Day gift from his grandkids or a Christmas present from his staff. But most often we acted and dressed with decorum.

Now that I am a free citizen, I occasionally shop in Chico's, where I can grab something garish. I don't always wear it, but I take it home as a closet brightener. I like the way Chico's gauges your body mass. You are a size 1, 2, or 3; there are no other choices. Under this new sizing system,

I'm no longer competing with those who wear a 6, 8, or 10; I have a number lower than they do.

When I was at the mall recently I had a flashback to the forties. During the halcyon days of summer, my mother and I would shop in the small dress emporiums along F Street in Washington, D.C. Professional saleswomen—pushy old broads who had been selling on commission for thirty years—would pounce on a customer, sometimes giving an elbow jab to a fellow worker trying to horn in.

Having established her territory, the salesclerk would smile pleasantly and offer her assistance. She would insist on taking your bags and storing them behind the counter to better facilitate your shopping experience. Worst of all, she would follow you around, suggesting outlandish garments for you to try on. I just wanted her to go away. But if I said anything, she would feign hurt and stand lurking on the other side of the rack, daring me to ask a question so she could rush over with more advice.

These purveyors of women's fashion all spoke the same language, as if they had attended the same sales-speak school. Here are some of my favorite lines. They are still used today, though most clerks lack the *savoir faire* needed to deliver them. The dialogue went something like this:

"Hello, my name is Thelma. How may I help you today?"

You insist that you are only looking. But she is undaunted.

"We just got in a lovely new shipment of jackets. Take a look at this one. Isn't it lovely?"

When I agree, she says, "Let me start you a dressing room."

I protest, but she assures me it's no problem.

"Try it on. This really looks cute on."

Before long, I'm trying on garments.

"*Oh, my lord! This is perfect on you!*" (Said with hands to mouth.)

She calls to a nearby saleswoman, "Come over here, Mona. Look at this. Have you ever seen a better fit?" Mona concurs and heads to the back room for a cigarette.

"Sweetheart, trust me on this, I've been in the business thirty years...*this* is your color. I wouldn't tell you this, if I didn't mean it."

Throughout the course of my indecision, she spouts more dressing room jargon.

"This is a very popular style this season. I sold three of these yesterday. You won't see this everywhere you go." These seem like two incongruous statements, but I leave them unchallenged. I allow for a little sales dementia on her part, as the lines are delivered five minutes apart.

The push is on. As I mutely evaluate the outfit in the mirror, she continues her monologue:

"Look at the detailing on the back of this garment. *It is gorgeous!*

"So flattering…and very slenderizing.

"You won't find anything like this for the price, my dear.

"You can wear it with anything. Very chic.

"I've got more sizes in the back…so just let me know."

She momentarily leaves me at peace, but returns cooing, "How are *we* doing in there? Do *we* need a different size? Come on out of the dressing room, dear. The light's not good in there. Come over here and look at yourself in the three-way mirror. It's a *purr-fect* fit! You could walk out of the store in this.

"If you don't like it when you get home, just bring it back and I'll give you a full refund."

As I start to show more interest, she begins to accessorize.

"This scarf (belt, shoes, earrings, bracelet) gives the outfit a whole new look. Very smart."

When I show concern about the price, she plays the economics card, "You get what you pay for, you know. This is a classic you'll wear year after year."

She pauses momentarily, hoping this will clinch the sale.

I fidget indecisively and begin to remove the jacket. Sensing she's about to lose a customer, Thelma plays her trump card. Putting her spectacles onto her nose, she eyes the garment tags, reflects for a moment, and whispers, "I can give you another ten percent off the ticket price. At that price, it's an absolute steal. I could be fired for giving away the merchandise."

When I express doubt about the fit, she dismisses my concerns with a wave of the hand.

"Honey, we can fix that shoulder...no problem...no problem...we do it all the time." Alternatively, she could have said: "It's a drop shoulder; it's supposed to fit like that."

Instead, she suggests we summon Ingrid.

"Ingrid is a miracle worker. She's been doing our alterations for years. She can tell you if a garment can be made to fit."

Ingrid appears with a tape measure around her neck, a red pincushion attached to her forearm, and a piece of tailor's chalk in her hand. Without a word, she sizes me up from all sides, tugs at the collar of my garment, pulls on the sleeve, and announces, "Yah, I kin fix. Ven do you vant?"

"Well, as soon as possible," I say sheepishly.

"I can git it for you in two veeks," she intones, as she begins to write my dimensions in her notebook.

"Two weeks?" I say in amazement.

"If you had come in last veek, I vas not busy. Theese veek, very busy."

Thelma begins the good-cop/bad-cop routine. "This is a very good customer, Ingrid [Thelma and I have never met before]; can you do any better than that?"

"You vant sooner? I git it for you next veek."

"Well, that's better," I say, still wishing it were sooner.

"Only few dollars more."

I sigh; I have already spent too much. I say, "I think the two veeks—I mean weeks—will be okay."

Ingrid disappears with my garment in hand.

Thelma is back in charge of me. I count out the cash into her hand, which is what we did in those days. She rings up my sale on the huge, ornate cash register with big keys that require some effort to activate.

"I will put a rush on this," she says with a wink. "Give me a call tomorrow."

With professional aplomb, she draws herself up straight, shakes my hand, and says with gusto, "It's been such a pleasure to serve you, my dear. Here's my card. I'm Mrs. Thelma Schwartz. The next time you're in be sure to ask for me. I'm here every Monday, Wednesday, and Friday, nine to five."

I Get By with a Little Help from My Friends

Each week, for nearly an hour, I put myself into the care of a hair therapist. Her license on the wall says *cosmetologist*, but we know better. She is well acquainted with my family, though they have never met. We share photos of vacations, weddings, and babies. We exchange home-grown tomatoes, magazines, postoperative stories, gossip, recipes, gardening tips, and sale locations at the mall. We have endured the ravages of time: she's still on her feet and I'm still showing up for my standing appointment even when the terrorist alert rises to bright orange.

Here's a woman who has cracked my hair color code, stocks my brand of conditioner, and still has a few cans of hair spray outlawed in the eighties for being too firm. She knows where my bald spots are and how to rearrange a few hairs here and there to make my coiffure more bountiful. She is more than a beautician; she is a magician.

When she mentioned that my hair was getting sparse around the temples, I explained that it was hereditary. My mother had the same condition. Mama just kept moving the back hair forward. It was not an attractive hairdo and I hoped I would not have to resort to it.

"What you need is a small hairpiece," she said. "It clips in place and covers the thinning area. I have one that I can color to match your hair for just ten dollars." Fool that I am for a few strands more of hair in the right places, I agreed.

Not long afterward I was in a coffee shop with Edna. We were talking about "community affairs"—who was having them and who was not—when she stopped abruptly.

"Hold on, honey," she said, "You've been spending too much time at the office. You've got a big paper clip trapped in your hair." With that, she flipped the hairpiece from my scalp.

"Oh, my lord!" she bellowed, when the hairy object hit the floor. "*It's alive!*" Edna jumped up and began stomping furiously on my new, ten-dollar hairpiece.

"Edna, calm down," I shouted. "It's just a hairpiece...or it was until you demolished it."

She reached down and picked up the lifeless chunk of hair with the bent clip.

"Oh, I'm so sorry," she said tenderly, handing me the remains with both hands as though she was picking up a pet from the side of the road. "I didn't know."

Then she became defensive. "You didn't tell me you were wearing a hairpiece. You would think that me being your best friend, I would be the first to know such things."

"Edna, it's no big deal. It's just a few strands of hair."

"What else haven't you told me?" she asked indignantly.

"Edna, you know everything about me...and I'm not sure that's a good thing."

"What exactly do you mean by that?"

"Every relationship needs some mystery. We'd be bored with each other if there weren't some surprises once in a while."

"Okay," she said, "surprise me with something I don't know. I'm feeling a little bored today."

I paused thoughtfully, trying to think of some tidbit to pacify my old friend. For a moment, Edna reminded me of the cartoon character, Witch Hazel, with her vow, "I warn you, dearie, I'm going to worm all your ugly secrets out of you."

Finally, I said, "Well, I've never told anyone, but I once took a store-bought pie to a home-baked dessert sale at the PTA."

"*You didn't!*" she said.

"Now you know the kind of person I really am."

"Did it sell?"

"That's the crazy part. It brought more than I paid for

it," I said. "That made me feel even worse."

"It was a fund raiser, for heaven's sake. Don't feel bad about that. What else have you been fretting about?"

"There is one thing that's been troubling me for some time," I said.

"Oh, tell me, honey, maybe I can help," Edna said, pulling her chair closer. "Just let it all hang out."

"Well, I've never told anybody, but the weight on my driver's license is wrong."

Edna furled her brow as best she could after having had three Botox treatments. "You didn't lie to the license clerk, did you?"

"It wasn't a lie decades ago. It's just that my weight has changed."

"How much are we talking about here…?"

"I think it reads 'a hundred and twenty pounds.'"

Edna sprayed her decaffeinated, mocha latte all over her silk pashmina. "Honey, we're talking a serious misdemeanor here. You could get six months to a year for that kind of violation. You'd better tell somebody and get that corrected right away."

"Now, how do you suppose I should do that?" I said. "I can't call up some guy at the license bureau and say, 'Can you help me? I need to change the weight on my driver's license to more accurately reflect my current size.' And he'd say, 'I'm sorry, madam, but unless you comply with the information we have on file, we will be forced to revoke your permit to drive. You have six weeks.'"

"Surely, he wouldn't say that. But if he did, it would be a great weight-loss incentive," she said. "Besides, I've always thought they should just put your dress size on your driver's license, like eight to ten, or twelve to fourteen. It gives you a little more wiggle room, so to speak. You might mention that the next time you're at the license bureau."

"I've shrunk an inch or more over the years, so my height is wrong, too," I added, "and my hair color has definitely changed."

"Well, your eyes are still blue," she said. "And your name's the same. I think you can make an argument that nearly half the information is accurate. If you need a character witness, you know you can count on me to vouch for you...though, I must say, that pie thing is troubling."

I'm an Ancient Explorer

It's not that I explore the ancient; I am an ancient who explores. A recent aggravation sent me on an exciting and revealing hunt. It all began when I got irritated with the pencils in my house. Each time I tried to use a pencil eraser, it smudged the paper and didn't remove the mark. I thought, "How could a company with the sole purpose of making pencils ignore the eraser portion?" Since I am one of the few who still uses a pencil, I set out on a quest to find the World's Best Pencil. After testing every brand at Home Depot and taking an unscientific survey of friends, I have reached a conclusion. My pencil choice is Ticonderoga 2HB Soft made from "premium cedar" and topped off with a "latex-free" eraser. Try it, you'll like it.

I am now testing root beer. I have long been a root beer devotee—a taste that I share with Snoopy, Dennis the Menace, and 3 percent of the soft drink market. But the beverage does not have the flavor that I remember from when I was a kid. I found out why. In 1960, the FDA banned the use of sassafras bark from the recipe, because of its carcinogenic properties.

Even so, I determined to find the best of the lot available. I am now working my way through the gourmet root beer section at Trader Joe's. So far, my pick is Virgil's—microbrewed, with no artificial ingredients or preservatives. The company makes an amusing comparison: what Ben & Jerry's is to ice cream and what Dom Pérignon is to champagne, Virgil's is to root beer. I have to admit, it's pretty doggone tasty. Not to be outdone is Fitz's, served on tap in a frosty mug—a favorite of St. Louisians, who take their root beer seriously. The search continues.

Besides exploration, I am doing the things that I'm good at, such as reading, shopping, traveling, phoning, advising, napping, grandmothering, and solving world problems. I am also trying to acquire some of the habits of the elderly, so no one will mistake me for being middle-aged. I now take the arm of a younger person when it is offered. I can make it on my own, but it makes them feel needed. I can give an "organ recital" of my ailments extemporaneously without being urged. I have developed patience and can listen attentively to strangers in the pharmacy line discussing the condition of their colon.

One good thing about the golden years is that you get to be as brassy as you like. You can say or do anything you please.

People will merely think you crotchety, senile, or eccentric. You can wear silly hats anytime, anywhere. Baseball caps, as John McCain does. Tyrolean hats with feathers and little hanging doodads. Or a Greek fisherman's hat that gives you the look of a European filmmaker. Slap anything on your head that covers bald spots or detracts from paunchiness.

I now give advice to my doctors. I criticize their magazine selections, their office decor, and their billing practices. I also suggest my own treatment, as I am slightly better acquainted with my body than they are.

Sometimes I lie to myself. For instance, I tell myself that the algae on my farm's pond looks like floating lily pads. That's almost true, when the sun hits the water just right. The subterfuge lessens the aggravation I feel from seeing the unsightly scum.

When someone makes a dippy remark, I smile and act as if I didn't hear it—which is not as hard to do as it once was. When an impatient motorist at the stoplight honks before I get myself in gear for the green light, I smile and wave vigorously in the rearview mirror as if we were old friends recognizing each other. After all, I'm in no hurry. I've already had the meat loaf plate with mashed potatoes at a restaurant that offers an Early Bird Special, and it's only 4:45 p.m.

My Cabernet Years

I am not just aging; I am fermenting like a good wine. In my Cabernet years, I am becoming more robust in opinion and definitely, more full bodied. In describing my life span, some cultures would say I have made seventy-seven rotations around the sun. I like that; the travel feature appeals to me. In China, I would be much older, because there you are one year old the day you're born and add a year with each January. I was born on December 20, which means that twelve days later I would have been two and looking terribly stunted for my age.

The Native American system racks up birthdays even quicker on its traditional lunar calendar. In that culture, I would be more than nine hundred moons old and subject to some young brave leaving me alongside the trail because I was slowing down the tribal migration.

Fortunately, my Scotch-Irish ancestors gave little heed to age. My grandmother just picked a number and stuck with it. She was fifty-five for at least a decade or until the need for Social Security overcame her vanity.

I like the thinking of the little girl who noted that her mother would soon be "thirty-eight...then thirty-nine.... then thirty-*ten*!" If life begins at forty—as we are told it does—by using this youngster's calculations, I would now be forty–thirty-seven, which sounds a lot better than seventy-seven or nine hundred.

Father Guido Sarducci, the comedian priest with the cigar and tinted sunglasses, has an even more fascinating suggestion for keeping track of your years. Instead of putting another candle on our birthday cakes each year, we should remove one. Insurance actuary tables tell us that the average life expectancy in America is about seventy-seven years. (At last, I've exceeded the average in something!)

Using Father Guido's system, we would start our celebration with a birthday cake of seventy-seven candles and remove one each year. When we get down to no candles on our cake, we become, not senior citizens, but Clean Cake People. Clean Cake People no longer blow out their candles— which is just as well, as it is increasingly more difficult over the years. Instead, they smear their hands through the icing and lick their fingers, giving evidence of a return to their second childhood. It makes a wonderful picture.

Because everyone from the Aztecs to the Zoroastrians has had a time-tracking system, I have mine. My premise, which I have modestly named Carnahan's Theory of Time and Locality, allows me to turn back my mental clock, if not the biological one. Whenever I observe my birthday on the other side of the equator or in another country, I deduct one year. According to my own calculations, I am now a mere sixty-eight years old and looking forward to further age-reducing celebrations abroad.

We always want to know the age of everything and everybody. Nature offers us some clues. We can tell the age of a horse by its teeth, a tree by its rings, ancient artifacts by carbon dating, and people by their wrinkles and sagging body parts. With horses, there are ways of filing their teeth to achieve a younger-looking mouth. With humans, age manipulation requires more creativity. If you can't afford a major surgical solution (or travel abroad), try some of these suggestions to at least appear younger to yourself and others.

1. Hang out with people half your age. Trying to keep up physically can be exhausting, so any association with the young should be done with caution and not for extended periods.

2. Hang out with older people. I know this seems like a contradiction of my first suggestion but, by comparison, elderly companions will make you feel younger and their activities will be less strenuous.

3. Appear to understand technology. Carry a BlackBerry or an iPad. Talk about gigabytes, URLs, uploading, and the number of friends you have on Facebook.

4. Brag about something you can still do at your age. I heard former secretary of state Madeleine Albright give a speech on the economic and political conditions in Eastern Europe and was amazed at how deftly she weaved in a segment about her leg-pressing capability.

5. Spend Saturday nights at the bowling alley rather than the bingo parlor.

6. Wear color—on your eyes, lips, hair, toenails, and in your jewelry and clothes. You might not want to do all of this at the same time, however.

7. Nothing says "old" like a low-information senior. Read the *Enquirer* to show that you are versed on who's Botoxing, childbearing, divorcing, and two-timing.

8. Never look down into a mirror. Gravity is not your friend.

9. Hire a personal trainer or sign up for a seniors' exercise class. It won't cure arthritis, but it gives you someplace where you can complain besides at home.

The Adventuresome Cook

Edna, Verna, and I had just finished our Morning Meet-up at the Mall, as we call it. We had completed our walk and our coffee shop visit was about to conclude.

"I've got to get home and put my roast in the Crock-Pot," Verna said.

"Hmmm...that sounds good," I replied.

"Oh, I get so tired of the same old thing. I wish I were a more adventuresome cook," Verna said.

"You need to be more like Marge Simpson. She said regular ham didn't thrill her anymore; she was crossing over to deviled ham. Maybe it's time you crossed over to something a bit more devilish," Edna advised.

"Like what?"

"Oh, you could start by putting red pepper flakes in your meat loaf," Edna teased.

"Seriously, what would you describe as adventuresome?" Verna asked.

"Well, there's sushi. Raw fish is always an adventure. And white asparagus is big nowadays. If you're eating out, you might try a tapas restaurant."

"Funny you should mention tapas," Verna replied. "The other night, my son said he was taking us to a tapas restaurant. I misunderstood what he said. And I shot back, 'Oh, no, you're not taking your father and me to any topless restaurant.' We had a good laugh and went to the topless—I mean tapas—restaurant and it was great fun eating all the little samples of food."

"I've noticed that some of the old foods are becoming trendy again," I said. "Every time I pick up a food magazine, there's a recipe for chicken potpie. My mother used to cook those all the time, but I haven't made one for years.

"SPAM is back—and I don't mean the Internet kind," Edna chimed in. "Now that was a meal in a minute. All you had to do was peel open the can with the attached key and you had the makings for breakfast, lunch, or dinner.

"Same thing with corned beef hash," I said. "My mother would open both ends of the can, push it out onto the counter, slice it into the frying pan, and it worked for any meal."

"Next thing you know we'll be serving that lime Jell-O

with pineapple and tiny marshmallows again. Or a tuna noodle casserole held together with cream of mushroom soup and sour cream," Edna laughed.

Verna ignored Edna as she often does and went on with her foods of yesteryear.

"I never see celery sticks stuffed with cream cheese anymore," she said with a touch of longing in her voice.

"No," I said, "but I have seen dates stuffed with a Boursin cheese and wrapped in prosciutto. Very tasty, but a lot more expensive."

"And what about succotash? When I mentioned the corn and lima bean combo at the table recently, my adult children looked at me as if I had just used a naughty word from the Urban Dictionary."

I remembered it well. It was one of those disgusting dishes in which the sweet corn masked the mealy, tasteless lima beans.

"My mother jazzed up our succotash with cream, butter, and nutmeg," Verna said, "but I could never pass it off to my grandkids. She also did a side dish she called 'stewed tomatoes.'"

"Yeah, I remember that," I said. "All you had to do was scrunch up a can of whole tomatoes into a pan, add some pieces of stale bread, seasoning, and sugar, and you had a primitive pizza. My mother added some bacon fat, too. She kept a can of leftover drippings sitting by the stove and added it to just about everything."

Verna said she thought food was a lot tastier years ago. "Nowadays they've taken all the fat and flavor out of home cooking. There are times when you need comfort food. Raw fish isn't going to do it for you like mashed potatoes and gravy."

"Raw fish isn't supposed to be comforting; it's supposed to give you a feeling of superiority," Edna said. "It's primeval and unadulterated."

"I don't know about that," I said. "They say it could be contaminated with mercury. But you never hear about root vegetables being chemically laced. That's pure, satisfying food."

"I'll drink to that," Verna said as she swallowed her last bit of coffee and headed toward the door. "I'll add a few potatoes and carrots to the Crock-Pot and Al will have the perfect caveman meal."

"Add some turnips, too," Edna shouted after her. "They're a bad-economy veggie and very chic nowadays."

That Takes the Cake

Most newlyweds don't have enough freezer space to store such items as the commemorative top layer of their wedding cake. Parents are entrusted with such responsibility. When this task befell me following the marriage of one of my sons, I dutifully wrapped and sealed the cake to preserve it for that magic moment—their first anniversary. I tucked it well into the bowels of the old, chest-style deep freeze in the basement, far from sight, in hopes that it would not be mistakenly thawed by someone in search of a sirloin tip roast.

My friend Edna warned me what would happen. She said that according to the statistical laws governing the first year of marriage, one or more of the following events would occur before the first anniversary rolled around:

1.   Couple separates or divorces.
2.   Couple moves to another state/country.

3.   One or both are on diet.
4.   Wife is hospitalized with first child.
5.   Freezer goes out during vacation.
6.   Parents die or move to condominium.
7.   Nephews find cake while looking for Popsicles.
8.   Cake saves the day at the family reunion.

Happily, none of those things had happened. I had a sense of satisfaction knowing that I had outwitted Edna with her doomsday predictions. When the anniversary rolled around, my son and daughter-in-law asked me to thaw out the cake in preparation for their visit. I put on a pair of gloves and headed for the basement. I lifted the freezer lid and leaned into the icy cavity, bending at the waist with half my body submerged in the frosty chamber. I discovered treasures long forgotten—a five-year-old elk roast, an unknown species of fish that Edna had given me when she cleaned her freezer, and a package of batteries that are said to survive longer on ice—but no cake.

In the spot where I had placed the cake, was a small, partially wrapped block about the size of a pound of hamburger. Now I allow for some freezer shrinkage, but this was ridiculous. When I picked up the loose wrapping, out rolled a small chunk of wedding cake covered with freezer burn. The rest had *disappeared*!

About that time, my oldest son walked down the stairs.

"What happened to Russ and Deb's wedding cake?" I asked, holding up the remains and the bundle of freezer wrap.

"Oh, is that what that was?" he said nonchalantly.

"You mean you ate all the cake they were saving for their anniversary?"

"Well, I didn't eat it all at once," he protested.

"But you ate it?"

"I guess you could say that. At first I just took small pieces because it was so hard to break off. You know, we've really got a good freezer there, Mom; it keeps food rock solid. I thought I would have to use a saline torch to break off a piece big enough to eat."

I was stunned. "How could you do this?" I asked.

"It was really hard. I eventually had to use a hacksaw and that was a lot of work."

The "cake-napper" later attempted to justify himself by explaining to his brother and sister-in-law that the cake had not maintained its original flavor and really should have been thrown away. He had spared them that discovery and given them the opportunity to make other arrangements. In time, the tale of the vanishing wedding cake became family legend and something we laughed about. And as I live in a family that always likes a good story—this one "took the cake."

I have since discovered that it's not the cake but the gift

that matters. An anniversary present is an absolute necessity for at least the first ten years. After that, orthodontia and motor overhauls take precedence. Here are some suggested gifts that every woman would love—I speak from experience here, having observed forty-six anniversaries. If you cannot afford the suggested item, use the alternative to show your heart's in the right place.

1. Love boat cruise with shopping stop in Puerto Vallarta. *Alternative*: A trip to the local marina, dinner at Captain D's with shopping at Walmart's Sale-a-Rama.

2. Trip to Las Vegas and big-star show. *Alternative*: Casino night at the local parish house; the ocarina player toots "Take a Chance on Me" when advised of the anniversary.

3. A larger, more visible diamond ring. *Alternative*: Replace the rings and pistons in the car. If there is still money left over, get her some new ring tones for her cell phone.

4. A fur jacket. *Alternative*: A zip-up snuggy bag from L.L.Bean.

5. A filmy, sensuous, negligee from Neiman Marcus. *Alternative*: His and her flannel nightshirts, monogrammed pockets, one size fits all, from the Sears catalog.

6.   A trip to some monumental site—Niagara Falls,
      Grand Canyon, Mount Rushmore. *Alternative*:
      A weekend bus trip to Branson, Missouri,
      with tickets to Andy Williams's Christmas
      extravaganza.

I could go on and on, but you get the idea. If you can't be
lavish, at least be imaginative. Or as some cheapskate once
said, "It's the thought that counts."

The Stars of Starbucks

One morning during an extended cold snap, Edna, Verna, and I ventured out to see one another.

"It's freezing outside today, so why aren't you wearing your heavy winter coat?" I said to Verna as we huddled around our cappuccinos at Starbucks. It had been a tough sell getting Verna to pass up Kelly's Koffee Kup, where she could get a decaf and Danish a lot cheaper, but she finally gave in.

"I don't wear that coat anymore," she said.

"Why not? It was an expensive purchase, as I recall."

"Well, I feel older when I wear it," she said sheepishly.

"So you're freezing your butt off, wearing a jogging suit today just to look younger to the Starbucks crowd?" I teased.

"I didn't want to come here, because I always feel so out of place without a computer," she sighed, pointing to all the latte laptoppers scanning the Internet.

Over at the Koffee Kup, they still read racing forms and day-old newspapers.

Now Verna is a lovely friend, who is normally unmoved by fashion and unfazed by innovation. She is still running the first version of Windows on an outdated computer her husband bought at a garage sale. She uses a Kodak Instamatic and has the film developed at the drugstore. Then she puts the pictures in an album, using those sticky, triangular corners, because she got a good deal on them years ago and still has a lot on hand. You might say Verna's a troglodyte. Once when I called her that, she responded, "No, I'm not and if I were, I wouldn't be talking about it in public."

Edna came to her rescue this morning. "Honey, if it makes you feel any better, just use my cell phone and pretend you're texting your broker."

When Verna brushed her off, Edna followed up with one of her folksy aphorisms. "Well, you know what they say: 'If you get stuck in the past, you'll get trampled by the future.'"

"That's a good line. Who said it?" I asked.

"I think it was Woody Allen...or maybe it was Woody Harrelson or Woody Guthrie—I forget which."

"I wish you'd get serious for a change. I have a problem here," Verna said.

"Well, dump it out on the table and we'll spill a little cappuccino on it and you'll never find it again," Edna said, trying to humor our old friend.

"I'm beginning to feel more and more out of touch," Verna said. "Take the TV commercials, for instance. They don't make sense to me anymore. I concentrate really hard but I can't always figure out what they want me to buy. I still don't get that Geico caveman commercial or the Capital One ad with the armadillo man."

Edna patted her on the hand to show her understanding. "Those ads aren't aimed at us, honey; we're not their target audience. For us, they play a catchy tune, because they know it will stick in our brain and we'll go around humming 'Viva Viagra' all the way to the drugstore."

Edna continued, "Then when the evening news comes on, I don't know a Shiite from a Sunni or the Taliban from al Qaeda or a…"

"Don't worry," Edna interrupted, "they're not sure themselves."

"But it's not only the television," Verna went on. "I even feel out of touch with my grandkids. I have a hard time deciphering those e-mails they send me. Their spelling is terrible."

Edna—who always has an answer—was on top of that one, too. "That's just their way of communicating today. Remember the speed writing we used to do back in high school? Every girl who couldn't make it in home economics had to learn shorthand and typing so she could support herself, since her homemaking skills made it unlikely she'd nab a husband. Besides, if you can read those abbreviated license plates that say goofy things in seven letters or less, you can decode your grandkids' messages."

About that time, a young woman walked passed our table, swigging water from a plastic bottle. "That's another thing I don't understand," Verna sighed pathetically. "Why is tap water only used for dishwashing, laundry, and bathing? Have you noticed that nobody drinks water today unless it's in a can, glass bottle, or plastic…and only if it is flavored or fizzy? I'm embarrassed to ask for just a plain glass of water anymore."

Before Edna could solve the tap water riddle, the woman with the plastic bottle started to leave. She put on her parka, wool hat, earmuffs, and scarf and shouldered her backpack. You'd have thought she was heading for an alpine slope instead of a heated SUV parked ten feet outside the door. She topped off her ensemble with *fingerless* gloves.

The three of us looked at one another dumbfounded.

Verna whispered, "I bet she paid more for those gloves without the fingers than I did for mine with them."

"That's not the point," Edna explained. "Her fingers are free to type exciting text messages on her BlackBerry and to operate the ATM, her XM car radio, and the credit card machines at the checkout counters.

"Verna, if you want to look 'with it,' my advice is to go home and put on your bulky coat and cut the fingertips off your wool gloves. Your hands might get a little more arthritic from the exposure, but at least you won't get a death of cold running around in that flimsy jogging suit trying to look forty-something."

"Well, you gals will be glad to know that I bought a birthday gift for Frank that is really cool and innovative."

"I think iPods are great. Is that what you got him?" Edna asked.

"No, he's got plenty of shoes," she replied. "I found this device in the Eddie Bauer catalog. It's a long, goose-down glove that has an ice-scraper handle built into the mitt with the blade extending out the end. Isn't that clever?"

"*Bravo!*" Edna shouted, clapping her hands excitedly.

I smiled. "Good thinking, Verna. "See, you're not a troglodyte after all. I think there's real hope for your becoming a techie."

Be Glad You Can't Read the Label

I am a compulsive reader. No print is too small or multi-syllabic for me to trip through. But I met my match some years ago when I was poking through the freezer. A frozen pizza propped against the door fell onto my foot. As I picked it up, I instinctively started to read the block of writing revealing its contents. On the Richter scale of print sizes, it was a miniscule six points and written in all capitals to decrease readability.

I expected a simple flour and yeast crust mixture topped off with tomatoes and cheese, so I was unprepared for the following disclosure of more than eighty-some different ingredients:

INGREDIENTS: CRUST *flour (wheat, malted barley), water, soybean oil, yeast, salt, dextrose, sodium aluminum phosphate, sodium bicarbonate, calcium propionate (preservative),* soy lecithin; **FILLING** whole milk mozzarella cheese (pasteurized whole milk, cheese cultures, salt, enzymes), ranch dressing (soybean oil, water, buttermilk powder, salt, distilled vinegar), blend of parmesan, romano, and granular cheeses (part skim cow's milk, cheese cultures, salt, enzymes, whey, lactic acid, citric acid, calcium chloride), egg yolks, sugar, phosphoric acid, garlic powder, natural flavors, onion powder, spices, sorbitol, corn syrup solids, maltodextrin, cultured nonfat milk, malt vinegar powder (with maltodextrin, food starch modified), sodium benzoate and potassium sorbate (preservatives), parsley, propylene glycol alginate, disodium inosinate, disodium guanylate, worcestershire sauce solids (molasses, vinegar, corn syrup, salt, caramel color, garlic, sugar, spice, tamarind, natural flavor), rice flour, rendered chicken fat, whey, yeast extract, lemon juice solids, xanthan gum, citric acid, lemon oil, oil of garlic, cooked white chicken meat (chicken breast with rib meat, water, dextrose, salt, modified corn starch) **SEASONING** maltodextrin, grill flavor (partially hydrogenated soybean and cottonseed oil), modified food starch, corn syrup solids, flavorings, soy protein isolate, sodium phosphates, spices, tomato, bacon (cured with water, salt, sugar, smoke flavoring, sodium phosphate, sodium erythorbate, flavoring, sodium nitrite), red onion, cheddar cheese (pasteurized milk, salt, cheese cultures, enzymes, annatto color), parmesan cheese (pasteurized part-skim milk, cheese culture, salt, enzymes, powdered cellulose (anticaking), cilantro. Contains 14% cooked chicken and 4.6% bacon.

Now, I'm not a purist when it comes to foods, though when I was in Korea I did reject the octopus tentacles served so fresh they were still moving on the plate. I don't want to eat anything that fights back. I also have an uneasy feeling about any product with ingredients I can't pronounce or contents that read like the fine print on a can of aerosol spray.

After my "pizza awakening," I began a campaign to introduce purer foods to the family table. The following week, I bought a small, frozen turkey breast. My teenage son, who by now was beginning to show some withdrawal symptoms from having been separated from chemically laced pizza for several days, examined the bird suspiciously.

"Foul," he cried.

"That's right," I said, "a wholesome fowl packed with protein, low in calories and fatty cholesterol. The perfect food."

"No, I mean *foul*, not *fowl*." [I didn't realize he knew the difference.] "This turkey has been injected with 'edible fat' and something called 'flavor enhancers,' and a bunch of chemicals identified only by initials. This is really gross."

He had a point.

Back to the store I went.

"Why can't I buy a simple unadulterated bird?" I said to the butcher.

"No flavor," he said. "People want flavor."

"Whatever happened to 'salt added to taste?'" I asked.

"Not good for you," he said. "Causes hypertension, water retention, and a bunch of things you don't want."

Meanwhile, my son had developed a plan to free us from antibiotic-injected poultry; he would bag a wild turkey in the woods behind our farmhouse. As I soon discovered, this undertaking required some planning and no little expense. In addition to roaming the woods before daylight to find where the turkeys were hanging out, there was the required turkey tag, camouflage gear, repairs to his old shotgun, ammunition, and the turkey caller. The latter device is used by hunters to produce a mating call that tricks a pea-brained turkey into coming out of the brush, thinking that a good time awaits him in the clearing. My son perfected his turkey talk enough to entice a large gobbler to come strutting into the open where he could get a clear shot.

We were spared the burden of dressing the bird (a euphemism for gutting poultry) when my son found a professional who performed this indelicate service for hunters, getting the turkey ready for the freezer in return for a few bucks.

I should point out that a wild turkey is not as plump as the shrink-wrapped Butterball that you pull from the freezer bin at your grocery. Store-bought turkeys have bent legs; a wild turkey's legs stick straight out like two exclamation marks. And the breast is flat, compared to the vitamin-fed birds raised commercially. Although I still enjoy a properly cooked wild turkey, I have not served one for several years. My huntsmen have taken up other pursuits, so I have returned to buying supermarket poultry.

"Do you want a bird that is fresh, frozen, organic, free-range, natural, kosher, a hen or a tom?" my butcher inquired the last time we talked turkey.

When I looked perplexed, he handed me a pamphlet to examine the various choices. I stepped back from the counter, joining several others who were reviewing the available birds and their characteristics.

"What do you think?" I said to one woman who appeared to have finished reading the fine print.

"Buying a turkey is a hassle." she said. "You have to order it ahead of time, come back and pick it up, and then find space for it in the refrigerator. I think I'm going to serve lasagna this year. My family's Italian so it will fit right in with our heritage."

"We're Irish," I said, "but I don't think I can get by with corned beef and cabbage for Thanksgiving."

She agreed. "Have you tried a turducken?" she asked.

"No, what's that?"

"It's all deboned meat. It starts with a turkey that is stuffed with a duck that is stuffed with a chicken. You just season the combo and pop it into the oven. A couple of hours later you take it out, slice, and serve. You can order it on the Internet."

Well, I ordered one that year. It was okay. But I missed bonding with the butcher. I missed wrestling with the icy bird on Thanksgiving morning and reaching elbow deep into the turkey hole, trying to fetch raw organs. I missed the family gathering in the kitchen to guess whether the twenty-four-pound turkey was done and to give their many opinions on what should go into the stuffing, how the gravy should be made, and who was skilled enough do the carving. I missed the turkey soup that comes several days later from cooking the bones with vegetables and noodles.

Edna says it's the fretting and worrying over the meal, the weather, and the attendees that makes Thanksgiving such a complex holiday. I guess that's why we observe it just once a year and follow up with a nap and football game.

The Senior Discount

"I'm starving. Where do you want to eat lunch?" I asked Edna as we drove along the highway, returning from our visit with a friend in the hospital. She was still munching on a piece of fruit scarfed from our sick friend's lunch tray.

"I don't care. Whatever you want is fine with me," she said.

"Well, what kind of food are you in the mood for?"

"Anything will do."

"That's not an answer, Edna. I've got to know which way to point the car. Do you want Mexican or Italian, Japanese or Vietnamese or Indian? Pick something."

"Why don't you pick the place this time?"

"You know I'm not a multitasker. I'm driving the car, for heaven's sake, and it takes all my concentration just to find the right lane. I can't be expected to pick the eating location, too."

"Well, when I picked the place last time, you didn't like the atmosphere."

"As I remember, the place was noisier than a World Cup soccer game."

"That's just because there was a busload of kids in there."

"I think a couple of those kids had a vuvuzela. Not only that, the waitresses moved as if they were wearing ankle weights."

"Jean, you don't call them waitresses anymore. They are servers. It's nonsexist language. Same for stewards and stewardesses; we now call them flight attendants. It makes you seem out of touch if you don't use the right terminology."

"Okay, okay," I said, "the servers were slow and it was loud, and the food was not memorable."

Edna reflected for a moment.

"Have you been to the new burger place at the mall—Five Guys with Fries?" Edna asked.

"It sounds greasy."

"It's lacking in ambience, but they give you free peanuts while you wait. All the burger toppings are free and there are refills on drinks. While you're eating, a cute guy in a red shirt comes over to your table to see if you're happy with your burger or need further assistance."

"I've been on a diet since this morning, so I'm thinking I need to eat something lighter."

"I thought you were hungry."

"Of course, I'm hungry. I'm on a diet."

"So you want a salad, right?"

"Probably," I said, realizing I had just limited my options by such a declaration. "How about a place with a senior discount?" I suggested, thinking the portions might be smaller.

"Good idea. I got my AARP membership packet this week and there's a list of places that give discounts to members."

"I didn't know you had finally admitted your age and joined up?"

"I held out for a long time; their magazine didn't have anything of interest to me. But in the last few years, the articles and ads seem to be a lot more relevant. I think they must have better writers."

I felt the same way and agreed that it must be the improved writing that made the difference.

"I just remembered, this is Tuesday," Edna said excitedly. "That means we can use my new senior discount card at Larry's Lunch Box."

That was fine with me.

A few minutes later I pulled into the crowded park lot at Larry's and started toward the first spot I saw.

"Don't take that space," Edna blurted out. "Go over there and look for one on the other side of the building."

"What's wrong with this space?"

"When I'm in a parking lot of a restaurant or big store, I only park on the left side of the building."

"What's that all about? Is this another one of your superstitions?" I asked as I passed up a perfectly good parking spot and headed for one on the far edge of the lot, but on the left side of the building.

"No, it's just that I used to 'misplace' my car in crowded park lots and I'd walk around aimlessly trying to locate it. Then I discovered that if I parked on the left side of a store, I only have half the space to search. I reduce my likelihood of loss by fifty percent. Does that make sense?" she said sheepishly.

"None whatever," I said. "But I'm hungry and don't have the strength to resist."

As we squeezed into the door at Larry's, I could see the place was packed with other bargain diners. When we were finally seated, I looked around to see what people were choosing to order on Discount Tuesday. As it turned out, the discount applied only to the senior lunch special, a meal that came with a salad, bread sticks, spaghetti and meatball (yes, just one meatball), beverage, and rice pudding, all for $4.50.

At a nearby table a group of young mothers was eating the baba ghanoush, a roasted organic eggplant dish mashed with tahini, garlic, and spices, served with pita bread. I noticed on the menu that it was nearly twice the price of the senior special.

When I questioned our server, he said the locally grown

vegetables appealed to the young women, many of whom were vegan. They would pay more for a simple, elegant dish rich in organic purity. But seniors wanted value and quantity, thus, the offer of a more traditional meal for a low price.

"Besides," he said, "our seniors like to have leftovers to take home."

According to our server, the vegan mothers collected their kids and cleared out by one o'clock, leaving the place to the decaf drinkers, some of whom hung around for a game of canasta in the side room. Our server also informed us that at one thirty, Larry would come out and play his accordion and take requests from the audience. It was worth waiting for, he said.

We didn't stay. But only because Harry had a dental appointment and likes Edna to come along. She says it has something to do with misery loving company.

Still, Edna was delighted at her discovery of Discount Tuesday at Larry's. "This is a senior discount you can get your teeth into," she declared, as she stuffed the remaining bread sticks into her purse.

But as we headed for the parking lot, she had a moment of "buyer's remorse." "I'm afraid we did some serious damage to your new diet by coming here today for the lunch special," she said apologetically.

"It was fine," I said. "No harm done. I only ate half the rice pudding."

Give Me a Sunny Sunday

Recently when I tugged on an overstuffed, seldom opened dresser drawer, its contents popped out like a package of Pillsbury biscuits. As it turned out, I had unleashed a treasure trove of old T-shirts back into the world. I lifted each one out and held it up as I read the wording, pondered the sentiments or admired the logo. Ahh…what memories.

"I could do a bio of my life with those tattered old tees," I told Edna when she stopped by my condo one fall afternoon to pick me up for lunch. Edna began to browse through the stacks of shirts with me. There were baggy shirts, stained shirts, shrunken shirts, and shirts with fluted edges and necklines that drooped below the collar bone.

"You were at Woodstock?" Edna asked, holding up a commemorative tee from the '69 rock festival, still in its plastic wrapper.

"For heaven's sake, no! I had just given birth two weeks earlier. I was having my own festival with three kids to see after. A friend sent me the shirt because she didn't want her mother to know she had attended the rock concert. I've been keeping it all these years in case she ever shows up wanting it back."

"There's a statute of limitations on such things. I think this could bring some cash on eBay."

"Perhaps so," I said, "Just put it in the 'Maybe' stack for now."

"The 'Maybe' stack?"

"Yeah, like I 'may be' keeping it or I 'may be' getting rid of it."

Edna rolled her eyes and tossed the shirt onto what was becoming the largest stack on my bed.

"What else do you have here?" Edna asked, looking at a photograph of a group of smiley-faced teenage girls imposed on a T-shirt that read BEST FRIENDS ALWAYS.

"Who are these people?"

I didn't recognize any of them.

"I have no idea, but it looks like we were having fun," I said, "so let's keep that one."

"Jean, you're a seventy-seven-year-old woman and I'm willing to bet dollars to doughnuts you'll never again wear this shirt."

"Sad but true," I said. "But, who knows, one of those gals might show up on my doorstep someday and remind me of a wonderful occasion we immortalized on that T-shirt."

As we slung shirts hither and yon, Edna couldn't resist

a running commentary on my collection. "It looks like you have a T-shirt for every place you've ever been and for every democratic candidate since Woodrow Wilson," she declared with some disgust in her voice.

"At least, this one might have some historic value," she added, as she unfolded my old JOHN KERRY FOR PRESIDENT shirt. "There's not much about that campaign to remember," she said, tossing it onto the "Keep" pile.

"I didn't know you climbed Pikes Peak," she said, holding up a lovely shirt featuring the Colorado crest.

"Well, it wasn't actually a climb in the usual sense," I said. "The family was on a three-generational vacation in a station wagon, pulling a borrowed camping trailer cross country. We were not a compatible lot. My eighty-year-old grandmother didn't like air blowing directly on her; it gave her neuralgia, she said. So that meant no open windows and only gentle air-conditioning.

"My father was a diabetic and prone to insulin reactions, so he had to be watched. And the dog had occasional bouts of car sickness that set off a chain reaction with the kids. There were at least two snorers in the trailer, so sleeping in the back of the station wagon with the luggage and the ice chest was the most desirable accommodations on the trip."

"So I take it, you want to keep this one?"

"No, not really. I don't need to be reminded of how to travel with a family of seven on less than thirty dollars a day.

I'm sure some kid in Haiti will think it's a cool shirt."

"What about this one from Thailand? It's kinda pretty."

"Hold on to that one. It fits perfect, has never faded, never stretched, and has gorgeous stitching. I've always wondered why we can't make a T-shirt like that here," I said folding it gently and tucking it back into the dresser drawer.

An hour and thirty-seven shirts later, we had several stacks: some for Goodwill, some to sell on eBay; but most to just pack away once again.

"What are you going to do with this 'Maybe' stack?" Edna asked. "It's getting pretty tall."

"I can't just throw them away," I protested, as I went through the pile a second time. "There're just too many memories. I can't even part with this old, tattered, tie-dyed shirt with a peace symbol on it that I hid from one of my kids because I was tired of seeing him wear it every day."

"Then give it back to him," Edna said.

"I'm afraid to give it back to him. He might put it on and wear it around town, or worse yet, my grandson might think it's trendy."

"A friend of mine turned her kid's old tees into a quilt and gave it to him for Christmas," Edna said. "She just cut out the front panels, framed each in a colorful fabric, and sewed them into a lovely coverlet of memories."

"Well, I guess that's better than turning them into dust rags."

"I don't know about that," Edna replied, "but, at least, it got them out of the closets and dresser drawers with less guilt. Besides, I'm not sure women of a certain age should be wearing a T-shirt emblazoned with pictures or dumb messages. We wouldn't be seen wearing stilettos or bikinis or sporting long gray hair, so maybe T-shirts should be off-limits, too."

"Now, here's one I might wear," I said, ignoring Edna's fashion analysis. "It's one I had made for my father: GIVE ME A SUNNY SUNDAY ANY DAY OF THE WEEK. He often looked out the window on a Sunday morning and said that—rain or shine."

"That's weird."

"No, it's not. My father was an optimist. He just liked every day to be bright and cheerful," I said as I slipped the shirt over my head.

It had a relaxed fit that felt good. I could almost hear my father voicing his Sunday sentiments.

"Okay, I'm ready for lunch," I said.

"You're not going to wear that goofy shirt out in public, are you?"

"Yep. Or maybe this purple one," I said, holding up a purple tee that read ED ASNER 4-EVER."

Edna heaved a sigh. "Well, at least, cover it up with a cardigan," she said.

In deference to my old friend's sensitivity to fashion,

I put on a sweater. No one noticed my T-shirt, but I did get a few compliments on my Halloween sweater with the sequined pumpkin faces and creepy spiders, dangling from loops of yarn.

Edna is so thoughtful. She said that the next time we lunched, she'd bring sandwiches and soup to my place. That way I wouldn't need to go to the trouble of getting dressed to go out.

If the Shoe Fits, They Won't Have Your Color

I was walking into a hotel one evening when I noticed that the woman ahead of me had red color on the bottom of her shoes.

"Look," I whispered to my daughter-in-law, "I think that poor woman has walked in some red paint. Do you suppose I should tell her?"

"No, no, don't do that!" she said quickly. "That's not red paint. That's Christian Louboutin's signature red-bottomed 'art for the foot.'"

"Art for the foot?" I exclaimed, "I can barely afford art for the wall and this woman wears it on her shoe soles."

"The shoes are Parisian—very chic and quite pricey," she added. "I'm sure she paid nearly a thousand dollars for them. All the celebs wear that brand: Beyoncé, Jennifer Lopez, Oprah. Some of the shoes are decorated with beading, colorful stones, and big bows. They come with animal-print heels, even furry toes."

Being as I am afflicted with cold feet, the furry toe part got my attention.

"My bedroom slippers have furry toes," I said. "I love them. I was wondering when someone would introduce that concept to outdoor footwear."

"What's more, they are all handcrafted," she added. "At least ten people touch them before they are completed."

"Well, I think you could say that at least ten, or more, people touch the shoes at Macy's before they're sold, but I've never heard anybody stress that point."

Still, I was glad she warned me about the red-bottomed shoes. Just imagine the conversation had I approached this woman with my concern for her shoe soles.

"Pardon me, but I couldn't help but notice that you have red color on your soles."

"Thank you," she would say smartly, beaming with pride at my recognition.

"I have a few Kleenex you're welcome to use if you'd like to clean them up before you step onto the carpet."

"Good idea," she'd respond. "They could use some polishing after walking on the dusty pavement."

Since the red sole incident, I've given more thought to footwear fashion. Sadly, with my bum knee and an artificial hip, I see no spiked heels in my future. I have no Manolo

Blahniks in my closet or even in my bank vault. Although I think that one of the floral, skyscraper stilettos would make a charming piece of art atop a pedestal in my entryway. As you can see, I'm not a shoey person; Imelda Marcos—with her 1,060 pairs of footwear—she's shoey.

As a youngster, I remember shopping at the Buster Brown and Mother Goose shoe stores. To make sure our little toes weren't cramped, we stuck our feet into a harmful X-ray machine that showed how our toesies were positioned in the shoesies. It was the highlight of the purchase. In that day, before the advent of Velcro, children's shoes had sensible laces and came in black or brown—or white, for summer. Come to think of it, so did shoes for women over the age of fifty. Life was simpler then.

Anything made of cloth was called a gym shoe, confined to the school locker, and pulled out to wear on the gymnasium floor only. With any luck at all, you could go an entire semester without bringing them home to wash. By the early sixties, mothers gave up polishing shoes and turned exclusively to washable canvas. From then on, we bought sneakers that lasted half as long as Buster Brown leather and cost twice as much.

Today the average woman has twenty pairs of shoes, but I limit my footrobe to no more than what will fit on my shoe rack. When a new pair comes on board, an old pair must shove off. Besides, I hate to buy shoes. There are only three shoe salesmen in all of America's shopping malls and they don't work on the days that I shop.

Salespersons spend a lot of time in the back room, pulling pairs off the shoe tree while you fidget, hoping the shoe gods will favor you with a fit. Shoe footmen also suffer from selective memory. They can retain your size, width, and all your style numbers and then forget where you are sitting. Although you only wanted to try on a pair of sandals that you pointed to on the display shelf, your salesman will return bearing a dozen boxes held in place by a well-trained chin. If you are twenty-something, he will hold your leg and insert your foot gently into your slipper; if you're wearing support hose, he tosses you a shoe horn and goes off to wait on another customer.

I am always amazed by what women will endure in the name of foot fashion. I see young cosmetologists who can stand all day in pointy-toed heels without flinching.

I inquired of one. "Honey, do you have shooting pains up your legs or numbness in your big toe at the end of the day?"

She smiled and asked if I'd like a cup of hot tea. She trotted off atop her stilettos and returned balancing a cup of hot water and an armload of magazines for my waiting enjoyment.

Our shoes used to give us away, but no more. There was a time when women of a certain age put aside their vanity and slipped comfortably into black, lace-up pumps with a "chunky Cuban heel" (a description Edna still uses to describe her ex-brother-in-law). Today the elderly can run around in tennies, wearing a heart monitor, and people will assume they have just left the gym rather than the cardiac rehab unit.

According to Edna, there are other ways of making a statement without wearing red-bottomed shoes.

"For the ecologically concerned, there is the trendy and socially responsible Cri-de-Coeur vegan footwear," she tells me. "The shoes are stylish, animal free, and cruelty free. The company plants a tree for every pair sold and purchases carbon credits to offset the emissions produced during manufacturing. By wearing vegan, you leave a green footprint in the world instead of a red one."

"But do they come with furry toes?"

"No, but they *are* edible in the event you get lost in the woods."

Keys, Eyeglasses, and Other Misplaceables

My father rattled when he walked. For as long as I can remember he wore a cluster of keys on his belt that made him look like a guard at Sing Sing prison. During a father-daughter moment, he revealed what he knew about each key. One—he thought—was to a house he lived in when he first got married. Obviously, that key had sentimental value.

Another opened a gate to his World War II victory garden. I could allow for a wartime trophy or two. Another was to a bank lockbox that held the family valuables: insurance policies, birth certificates, and a five-dollar gold certificate that was supposed to be turned over to the federal government in 1933, when the country went off the gold standard. By far, the most intriguing were the skeleton keys that could unlock cabinetry and a variety of door locks used until the late forties.

I am now more understanding than I once was of key carriers. I think of my father each time I stir the contents of my purse in search of my own collection. If I just had the nerve (good sense, stamina) to wear them on my person, I would save a lot of bottom fishing. I should attach my reading glasses and cell phone to my person, too, but I worry about looking like the condo maintenance man.

Edna says I'm a loser. Now, I don't think she means that in a derogatory sense. She's just describing my tendency toward misplacement. For years she has encouraged me to wear my reading glasses on a chain about my neck. I have refused. Nothing says "senioritis" like a woman's spectacles resting upon her bosom, vying for space with her SARAH PALIN 2012 button or getting entangled in her necklace that features the birthstones of her eight grandchildren. Besides, a neck chain reminds me of the strings that once ran down my arms to hold my mittens in place.

So I constantly pursue my readers. I can misplace a pair or two a day. Then again, I once hit the jackpot when I was cleaning under the driver's seat of my car and out tumbled three pairs.

One day after Edna had loaned me her reading glasses, she said thoughtfully, "Might I make a suggestion?"

"You've never been reluctant to do that before," I responded.

"What you need are Smart Goggles, the eyeglasses with a mini camera and computer built into the frames. You walk around the house and it films everything you look at and stores the location in its computer. It's perfect for the forgetful, the careless, and the clueless."

"What happens if you're dumb enough to lose your Smart Goggles?" I asked.

"That would be a problem for a person such as yourself. You need RFID. My dog has RFID," she said.

"I thought your dog was looking puny the last time I saw him."

"You don't even know what I'm talking about, do you?"

"Sure I do. You're talking about that terrible stealth ailment that overtakes those in the prime of their retirement years: rheumatism, fungus, irritable bowel syndrome, and dementia—RFID."

"I'm talking about the radio frequency identification tags. It's a microchip put into clothing, electronics, and anything that manufacturers want to track. They can also be implanted into dogs and cattle—and potentially teenagers. It's just a matter of time before we can have RFID tags attached to any personal items we have trouble keeping up with. Think what it would mean not having to meander through the parking lot, acting as if you know where you left your car."

"I see a problem here," I said. "We can keep in shape

with pacemakers, hearing aids, contact lenses, hip and knee replacements, hair transplants, and Botox treatments. Now we have these microchips to assist failing memory. How will we know when we've grown old?"

She reflected momentarily. "Age is a state of mind," she declared with the air of a seasoned gerontologist. "There are several measures of aging. Hold on a minute; I can determine your condition with a simple test."

With that, she opened her purse and took out a folded page that she had obviously torn from a magazine at the doctor's office and began reading to me about the Geezer Gauge.

"Geezer Gauge? What in the world are you talking about, Edna? This is ridiculous," I protested.

"Just stick with me here. I want you to answer these five questions, so I can determine just how close to geezerhood you are. Question number one: Do you stay in your housecoat and slippers until lunchtime?"

"I don't even own a housecoat. Does a jogging suit qualify?"

"Okay, that's good. Do most of your companions have MD after their name?"

"Well, too many of them do, but I think that's a good sign. I'm caring for myself. Besides, I give my physicians a free political consultation with each visit. If you just let 'em be, they'll turn into Republicans every time."

"Don't get started on that…the next question is: Do you sometimes forget to ask for the senior discount?"

"Yes, and it makes me mad as hell when they give it to me without my asking."

"All right, question number four: Do younger people greet you warmly, take both your hands into theirs, and marvel at how good you still look? "

"They do. But I always thought it was because they were jealous."

"Final question: Do you wear a bra?" she asked.

"*Edna!* That is a very personal question."

"Actually, it's a very poignant question," she replied, "one that tells a lot about your age."

"Okay, I wear a bra. So what does that mean?"

"Ah-ha!" she replied. "Today it's young women who go braless; no longer older women. So, by wearing a bra, you are showing your age."

"I'd be showing a lot more if I didn't," I said disgustedly. "I've had enough of this. I'm through with your senior assessment."

"Hold on, there's a bonus question that might help your score. Do you think this joke is funny: One elderly woman leans over to her friend and whispers, 'I'm having an affair.' The other responds, 'Really! Are you having it catered?'"

"So, what's the punch line?" I said, trying as best I could to keep a straight face.

Edna threw up her arms. "I give up," she said. "Now you've gone and lost your sense of humor, too. As best I can tell, you have another six to eighteen months before you qualify for geezerhood."

"Great!" I said. "Let's hit the mall while we still have some time left."

Your Feet Stink

The toughest negotiators are not to be found in corporate boardrooms or political back rooms, but under our own roofs. It is those pint-size tyrants—our children—who know how to stick it to us and when.

I was reminded of this recently as I sat in a restaurant next to a woman and her three- to four-year-old daughter. When the waiter appeared to take their order, the conversation went something like this:

"Sweetheart, what would you like for lunch?"

The youngster, happily occupied with blowing bubbles in her water glass, ignored the question.

"Mommy is talking to you, Sarah Ann. Would you like to have grilled cheese or a hamburger or a tuna fish sandwich?"

"Noooooo. I would like a goo-goo burger," she said throwing her head back and giggling with glee. "I want a goo-goo-gooey burger."

"What in the world is that?" her mother asked.

"I don't know…but that's what I want."

The waiter shifted his weight to his other foot, smiled patiently, and said they were out of "goo-goo gooey burgers."

"Come on now, Sarah Ann, tell the nice waiter what you want to eat."

"I want a…I want a…I want a big, big, big, *big*, BIG Crayola sandwich with ketchup," she laughed.

As I was leaving, little Sarah Ann had just turned her nose up at the peanut butter and jelly special and was arguing that they move on to McDonald's. The last I heard was the mother's soulful plea, "But, Sarah Ann, you said you wanted to eat here."

As I paid my bill, I recalled a sign I once saw in a restaurant that apparently had one too many Sarah Anns bounding about the tables. It read: "We love kids, but please keep yours at your table. Unattended kids will be given a shot of espresso and a free puppy."

Now, I don't mean to be too hard on Sarah Ann or her mother. With four children to manage, my family didn't eat in restaurants that often, but we did get in and out of the station wagon a lot. It was a tricky maneuver requiring patience and stamina on the part of the adult passengers. I can recall my children shuffling for position before they ever left the house.

"I'm getting in first."

"No, I'm getting in first."

"You got in first last time."

"You sat by the window last time, so it's my turn."

"I don't want to sit next to you. Your feet stink."

"My feet don't stink. You take that back…or I'll…."

When my father-in-law was traveling with us, he quickly took command. He was something of an authoritarian, who would never think of asking a child a complex question such as, "Where do you want to sit?" or "What do you want to eat?" Just as the bickering got under way, he would appear on the scene, make a quick assessment of the situation, and begin to mete out seating assignments like a hardened Southwest Airlines' agent.

"You sit there…and you sit next to the window…. and you sit in the middle. You squeeze in next to him. And the dog goes right there on the floor." Without further ado, they would pile in, not always happy but resigned to their fate.

"Now, is everybody happy?" he would ask. They would all nod their heads agreeably. "Okay, then, I don't want to hear another word about seats." It was much like packing eggs into a carton; when he was through, we all felt snuggly in place and ready to be transported to our destination.

After he died, we reverted to our barbaric practice in which the strongest, loudest, most persistent prevailed. The backseat badgering commenced before we were out of the driveway.

"He's standing on my hair."

"That's because you put your hair under my foot."

"Mom, she's hogging all the air."

"I'm not hogging…I'm just breathing. You want me to stop breathing?"

"Sure, go ahead."

"Mom, he's putting his wet finger in my ear again…You are so gross…Don't look at me ever again."

"You want gross, this is gross…"

I glance in the rearview mirror to get a glimpse of the grossness of which they speak, but I nearly sideswipe the car in the next lane.

"Mom, he's looking at me that way again."

"You are such a wimp and a tattletale."

"I'm not, either."

"You are, too.

"Mom, he called me a bad word."

"No, I didn't. You said it first."

When I reached the end of my rope, I would make some lame threat, "If you don't settle down back there, I'm going to stop this car and put all of you out on the side of the road."

"If you're going to do that, drop me off on the next corner so I can walk to Larry's house and shoot some baskets."

"No, I'm not letting you off anywhere. You have to stay right here in this car."

"I thought you wanted to let us out."

"Not on your life, young man, you're going to stay in here and suffer along with me."

I try to determine the culprit.

"You...no, not you—you with the hair," I say, looking into the rearview mirror, "crawl up here and sit in the front seat with me right now."

"Who do you mean? We all have hair."

"You know who you are," I say pointing at the one with the overdue haircut.

"I can't move; I'm squeezed in too tight."

"You can't move because you're too fat. Here...let me give you a shove."

"Ouch! You didn't have to poke me with your bony elbow."

The move to the front seat is accompanied by the flailing of arms and legs. During the scuffle, the dog finds refuge in my lap.

In desperation, I pull over, stop the car, and deliver a stern talk on auto safety and passenger civility. That usually bought me enough time to make it to the grocery store parking lot.

Some forty years later, I got into a car with an acquaintance who has three children. I had a "battlefield" flashback like a veteran with post-traumatic stress disorder. To my surprise, these youngsters climbed quietly into the backseat, adjusted their seat belts, and immediately attached themselves to an iPod. We had a blissful ride with no unseemly outbursts—though I did overhear one familiar theme that stirred my memory.

"Move your feet over," one whispered to the other, "they smell."

"So do yours, only worse."

You Might Be Getting Old If...

Edna, Verna, and I were finishing off a bottle of wine when our creative juices kicked in. We were discussing how to tell whether you're old.

"Age is not a figure anymore," Edna declared. "There are lots of other things to factor in."

Well, one thing led to another and before long we had come up with a list of surefire age indicators. It's our version of Jeff Foxworthy's "How to Tell If You're a Redneck."

If you think old age is sneaking up on you, check yourself out against our list.

You might be getting old if...

1. The grocery clerk offers to help you to the car when you have only one small sack.
2. You are given the senior discount at the theater without asking.

3. You start getting mail from nursing homes, the AARP, and funeral directors selling advance burial plans.

4. People hold your hand and speak directly and distinctly into your face.

5. Upon greeting you, people tell you how good you look, with surprise in their voice.

6. Your friends keep having surgery or dying, making it impossible to put together a table of canasta.

7. You don't stand naked in front of a full-length mirror anymore.

8. Most of your acquaintances have MDs after their names.

9. Soldiers look like little boys and girls to you—same for doctors, dentists, ministers, and financial advisors.

10. You turn up the volume during the commercials to see if your symptoms match those of the new diseases they're advertising.

11. You jot things down just in case, then lose the note that you put someplace so you wouldn't forget it.

12. Your pharmacist is your new best friend.

13. You pay less attention to whether an appliance has a lifetime guarantee.

14. You have a wardrobe of wrinkle-free polyester that frees you from worrying if you left the iron on when you leave home.

15. You are less reluctant to park in the handicapped spot, because anyone over seventy qualifies on some level.

16. The salesclerk says the item of clothing that you're trying on makes you look ten years younger.

17. You become highly irritated when they stop making your lipstick shade, bra style, or hair color; drop the meat loaf entrée from the menu of your favorite restaurant; or your doctor dies, moves, or retires—same for hairdressers/barbers, ministers, repairmen.

18. You regularly doze in front of the television and computer; at church, musical performances, and family gatherings; in cars and waiting rooms; and after meals.

19. Colorful protuberances grow on your skin and need to be removed like barnacles from a ship's hull. Hair falls out, sticks out, or grows out of the wrong places. All of this is nature's payback for making fun of your wrinkled, bewhiskered great-aunt.

20. You don't know how to operate the fancy features on your television, recorder, camera, car, cell phone, oven, or Windows 7.

21. You give spontaneous and unsolicited advice to store clerks, grandchildren, in-laws, strangers, and others you deem needy.

22. You are annoyed when you forget why you dislike a person that you've disliked for years.

23. You can tell the same bit of family lore more than one way, depending on the audience and the point you're trying to make.

24. People no longer laugh at your jokes. They smile sweetly and pat you on the hand.

25. When you talk about past events, you have to do a quick mental calculation to see if your listener is old enough to share your recollections.

26. You no longer care about your cholesterol level. You must be doing something right or you'd never have lived this long.

27. You give your doctors free advice on health, politics, magazine subscriptions, and billing procedures.

28. Tying shoestrings, carrying groceries, changing an overhead lightbulb, and walking the dog around the yard are classified as exercise, as is

retrieving anything from under the bed, back of the closet, or the lower kitchen cabinets.

29. You've been spotted several times leaving the house with unmatched socks or shoes.

30. You ask what day it is more than once a day.

31. You still take your favorite green Jell-O mold to a church potluck supper.

32. Your children and friends often tell you that your makeup is smudged or your lip liner uneven, and there's a growing collection of stains on your favorite blouses.

33. Your cat's hysterectomy was the highlight of your Christmas letter.

34. You're at peace with the realization that your abs will never again be concave.

35. You're needlepointing a likeness of Sarah Palin onto an American flag background as a gift for your granddaughter.

36. Your family stands by with a fire extinguisher as they light your birthday cake.

37. You still prefer AAA TripTiks to the GPS your kids gave you for Christmas.

38. You are among the only three to attend your class reunion and you don't recognize the other two—not even their names—and wonder why the hell you bought a new outfit.

39. You forget who's dead and who's alive and will argue about someone's existence.

40. When you say things like, "Seventy is the new fifty," people nod agreeably, but really think you're losing your cognitive reasoning. (Although I have a thirty-ish friend, who declares that "thirty is the new ten." She says it gives her an excuse to buy more expensive toys.)

41. Your family asks your advice on gardening, but not child rearing; baking from scratch, but not clothing or hairstyles; family genealogy, but not whom to marry.

42. You know all the words to the music playing in the elevator and at the dentist's office.

43. Waiters at banquets automatically pour you decaf coffee.

44. You've eaten the same thing for breakfast for the last twenty years.

45. At the antique car show, you recognize all the makes and models and which ones you drove, the gas mileage, and your monthly payments.

46. Your weightlifting now consists of getting your body out of bed in the morning.

47. You'll wear any ridiculous hat as long as it shields your face from the sun.

48. You have unexplainable aches and pains after

doing nothing more strenuous than watering the grass or lifting a roast from the oven.

49.   You don't recognize anyone in *People* magazine.

50.   You've turned all your sleeveless tops into dust rags.

51.   You are the only one in your family who says, "Oh, shucks."

52.   You would like to buy some recordings, but you can't find a record store.

53.   You've never heard of the Urban Dictionary.

54.   You think Twitter is what birds do.

55.   You don't jump into bed anymore—or into the car or the shower. You ease in.

56.   You get aggravated because household devices no longer have a simple button marked ON/OFF.

57.   All your luggage has wheels rather than backpack straps.

58.   It takes several days before you discover you failed to reset your clocks for daylight saving time.

59.   You have a doctor for each of your afflictions.

60.   The hair on your grandkids bothers you more than the hair in the sink.

61.   When you enter a room of young people, they go into a respectful "geezer mode" of conversation.

62. People around you talk about the weather and their bowel habits a lot more.

63. You know the location of all the bathrooms in the mall, local restaurants, public buildings, and airports and can give an evaluation report on each.

64. You keep more things by your bedside...in your purse...in the trunk of your car...in the freezer and the medicine cabinet—just in case you might need them.

65. You still dress up when you go to the doctor, fly on an airplane, or attend church.

66. You reread books because they seem like old friends.

67. You still can't bring yourself to wear white after Labor Day.

68. You went to the Pocono Mountains on your honeymoon and have the pictures organized in slide trays.

69. Your baby photos are in black and white.

70. You still have a set of encyclopedias on your bookshelf.

71. You once had avocado carpeting in the living room, linoleum in the kitchen, or knotty-pine walls in the rec room.

72.   You have neither the verbal skills nor the
      inclination to use the f-word three times in
      one sentence.

73.   You ask a guest, who mistakenly sits in *your*
      chair, to move to another seat.

74.   Your cell phone melody is "Star Dust."

75.   You keep jars of hard candy in the house all year
      round.

76.   You still have a Kodak Instamatic.

77.   You keep a space heater in the bedroom and
      bathroom for all but three months of the year.

78.   Your kids don't understand the benefits of
      silk plants, vinyl seat coverings, and polyester
      T-shirts. But they do enjoy the convenience of
      plastic water bottles, plastic wrap, and credit
      cards.

79.   For Christmas, you knit matching scarves for the
      entire family and the dog.

80.   You once had a parakeet named Tweetie Pie.

81.   You buy your good jewelry on QVC.

82.   When you wear mismatched or unmatched items
      of clothing, no one mentions it anymore.

83.   You apply your makeup with a spackling knife.

84.   When you stoop over to pick something off the
      floor, you think, "Is there anything else I need to
      do while I'm down here?"

85. You can hide your own Easter eggs.

86. You remember when *night out* meant sitting
     on the patio in the evening, *getting lucky* meant
     finding a parking space, and *going all the way*
     meant staying on the transit to the end of
     the line.

87. You once owned a Studebaker.

88. People call at nine p.m. and ask, "Did I wake
     you up?"

89. At breakfast you hear "snap, crackle, and pop"
     and you're not eating cereal.

90. You recall when people could smoke on a plane,
     in an elevator, and the doctor's office.

91. You once wore a stiff crinoline petticoat to make
     your long ballerina skirt swish when you walked.

92. Your childhood wardrobe consisted of play
     clothes, school clothes, and Sunday clothes, and
     none of your toys required batteries.

93. You remember when married couples in films
     always slept in separate beds.

94. You bought your toaster with S&H trading
     stamps.

95. You once had a car that had a metal dashboard,
     ashtrays at every seat, a running board, and three
     on a tree, but no seatbelts or airbags.

96. Your joints now give you a more accurate

barometric reading than the National
Weather Service.

97. You have fond memories of Jack Webb.

98. You still use any of the following words:
tomfoolery, poppycock, nincompoop, piffle,
hogwash, dadgumit, lollygagging, doohickey,
or groovy.

99. You remember when cooling the car meant
rolling down the windows.

100. And, you might be getting old if you have
nothing better to do than read this book.

ACKNOWLEDGMENTS

No, Virginia, there is not an Edna or a Verna. But there are many wonderful friends, family members, and co-workers who patiently read these vignettes, improved upon some, and suggested that others be gently deleted to the trash bin of memory.

My real friends have unwittingly provided the inspiration for the lovable antics of my fictional friends, Edna and Verna. While they may not want to be outed as accessories to my "crime" of storytelling, that's the risk they've taken as my friends.

Although they range in age from thirty- to eighty-something, they're all young at heart. During the years it took to create *A Little Help from My Friends,* we have lifted many a fork and glass and enjoyed the benefits of hearty laughter. Like Monty Python's Black Knight, we have endured a few flesh wounds, but refused to yield to time and troubles.

I have borrowed upon the genial spirits of such dear

friends as Inda Schaenen, Lucy Sutcliffe, Corrine Beakley, Cyndy Crider, Judy Aronson, Summer Johnson, Barbara Eagleton, Ethel Burton, Oma Carnahan, Wilma Turner, Sonia Pendergrass (deceased), Ruth Ann Phillips, Sheila Goldstein Small, Nina Ganci, Wendy Werner, Judy Dean, Jane Albrecht, Barbara Gilby, and Laura Swinford.

What a great time we've had figuring out life.